LEO XIV:
Portrait of the First American Pope

MATTHEW BUNSON

Portrait of
THE FIRST AMERICAN POPE

LEO XIV

EWTN Publishing, Inc.
Irondale, Alabama

Copyright © 2025 by Matthew Bunson.

Printed in the United States of America. All rights reserved.

Cover design: Emma Helstrom

Cover image: Vatican (Unsplash from Caleb Miller - milljestic); close-up of textured white paper (1155801527), derived from Thak Pixel / stock.adobe.com; Pope Leo XIV (2213412056), derived from TIZIANA FABI / gettyimages.com

Papal Coat of Arms: Papal coat of arms Leo XIV Sodacan Style.svg (Creative Commons Attribution-Share Alike 4.0 International)

No part of this book may be reproduced, stored in a retrieval system, or transmitted in any form, or by any means, electronic, mechanical, photocopying, or otherwise, without the prior written permission of the publisher, except by a reviewer, who may quote brief passages in a review.

EWTN Publishing, Inc.
5817 Old Leeds Road, Irondale, AL 35210

Distributed by Sophia Institute Press, Box 5284, Manchester, NH 03108.

paperback ISBN 978-1-68278-437-2

ebook ISBN 978-1-68278-438-9

Library of Congress Control Number: 2025939757

2nd printing

SPA POD 2025

Dedication

This book is dedicated to my wife, Bonny Bunson.

Indulgenced Prayer for the Supreme Pontiff by Pope Leo XIII

O LORD, IN UNION with millions of believers, and prostrate here at Thy feet, we pray Thee to save, defend, and long preserve the Vicar of Christ, the Father of the glorious society of souls, our own Father. Today and every day he prays for us, fervently offering to Thee the sacred Victim of love and peace. Turn then, O Lord, Thy loving eyes upon us, who forgetful as it were of ourselves pray now above all things for him. Unite our prayers with his, and receive them into the bosom of Thy infinite mercy, as a most sweet perfume of that living and efficacious charity, in which the children of the Church are united to their Father. All that he asks of Thee today we too ask for with him. Whether he sorrows or rejoices, or when he hopes or offers the Victim of love for his people, we would be united with him. We desire that the utterance of our souls should be one with his. Mercifully grant, O Lord, that no one of us be far from his mind and heart during the hour of his prayer, and when he offers to Thee the sacrifice of Thy blessed Son. And in the moment that he, our most revered Pontiff, holding in his hands the very body of Jesus Christ, shall say to the people over the chalice of benediction the words: The peace of the Lord be ever with you, do Thou, O Lord, cause Thy most sweet peace to descend with a new and manifest power into our hearts, and upon all the nations of mankind. Amen.

— *The Raccolta, 1910 ed.*

Acknowledgments

THERE ARE MANY INDIVIDUALS to whom special thanks are owed in the completion of this book:

Michael Warsaw, Chairman of the Board and CEO of EWTN, for his confidence, especially that this project could be completed in an expeditious manner. Montse Alvarado, President and COO of EWTN News, for her enthusiastic support. Andreas Thonhauser, Vatican Bureau Chief and the remarkable members of the Vatican Bureau in Rome who worked so tirelessly during the *sede vacante*.

I am also grateful for the unfailing support of Devin Jones and Taylor Wilson of EWTN Publishing, and I am deeply thankful for the immense help of Brandon McGinley.

Finally, my thanks to my wife, Bonny, for her boundless patience over the days spent in the preparation and writing of this book.

Contents

Dedication v
Acknowledgments vii
Foreword xi
Introduction: Destined for Greater Things 3

PART 1
CHICAGO: CITY OF THE BIG SHOULDERS

1. An American Upbringing 17
2. Witness to Decline 29
3. Son of Augustine 39

PART 2
PERU: LAND OF CONTRASTS

4. Padre Roberto 57
5. Christ in Peru 67
6. A Missionary's Heart 79

PART 3
ROME: THE ETERNAL CITY

7. An Experienced Churchman 89
8. The Conclave 103
Conclusion: A New Leonine Age 113
Afterword 123
Endnotes 129
About the Author 137

Foreword

"Peace be with you all!"

On the afternoon of May 8, 2025, tens of thousands of people gathered in St. Peter's Square waited with excited anticipation for the verdict of the Cardinal Electors gathered in the Sistine Chapel. It was the second day of the conclave to choose a successor to Pope Francis, and three inconclusive votes had already been taken, signaled by the black smoke that had poured out of the temporary chimney attached to the roof of the Sistine. The fourth vote — the first of the afternoon — should have happened by then, and if inconclusive the cardinals would have moved onto the fifth vote, whose ballots would be burned to produce smoke, either white or black.

Suddenly, however, at 6:08 p.m. Rome time, the crowd erupted as white smoke began issuing from the chimney: The cardinals in the conclave had chosen the 267th pope in the history of the Church. As it happened, the election did occur on the fourth vote, and the ballots were burned according to the rules of the conclave to produce white smoke.

As the sun began setting on the city of Rome, the doors behind the main loggia of St. Peter's opened and the senior cardinal deacon, the protodeacon, Cardinal Dominique Mamberti, announced in Latin:

> Annuntio vobis gaudium magnum; habemus Papam! Eminentissimum ac Reverendissimum Dominum, Dominum Robertum Franciscum Sanctae Romanae Ecclesiae Cardinalem Prevost. Qui sibi nomen imposuit LEONEM XIV.
>
> I announce to you a great joy: We have a pope! The most eminent and more reverend lord, Lord Robert Francis Cardinal of the Holy Roman Church Prevost. Who has given himself the name LEO XIV.

The announcement came as a surprise to the throng in the square, with their surprise turning to shock around the globe as the realization came that Cardinal Robert Francis Prevost, a native of Chicago, Illinois—an American—had been elected the 266th Successor to St. Peter and had taken the name Leo XIV.

A short time later, Pope Leo XIV walked out onto the loggia to deliver his first apostolic benediction, *Urbi et Orbi*, "To the City and the World." He paused briefly for a moment as he was overcome with emotion, and then he said his first words as pope, in Italian: *La pace sia con tutti voi!* ("Peace be with you all!")

He went on:

> Dear brothers and sisters, these are the first words spoken by the risen Christ, the Good Shepherd who laid down his life for God's flock. I would like

this greeting of peace to resound in your hearts, in your families, among all people, wherever they may be, in every nation and throughout the world. Peace be with you!

It is the peace of the risen Christ. A peace that is unarmed and disarming, humble and persevering. A peace that comes from God, the God who loves us all, unconditionally.[1]

In his *Urbi et Orbi*, the new pontiff spoke in Italian, Spanish, and Latin. But he began with words that have already formed the heart of his young pontificate: "Peace be with you all!"

Pope Leo XIV arrived at the papacy at the age of sixty-nine with a plea for peace after long decades of service as a priest, a missionary, a bishop, a cardinal, and a dedicated member of the Augustinian Order. He had served in the United States, in the missions and dioceses of Peru, and in Rome. He was chosen on the fourth ballot of the conclave to succeed Pope Francis by the largest and most diverse body of cardinal electors in Church history—who chose the first U.S. born pope, the first North American, and the second consecutive pope from the Americas.

In his plea for peace, Pope Leo XIV expressed his desire not just for peace that spans the cultural, political, socioeconomic, and ecclesiastical divides in the world and the Church, but authentic peace, the peace, as he said, of the risen Christ.

He was chosen by the cardinals in the conclave because he is a bridge-builder to authentic peace, in keeping with the traditional title and symbol of the papacy—pontifex. As Cardinal Timothy Dolan said of his election, "It should not startle us that we would look to Pope Leo as a bridge builder. That's what the Latin word 'pontiff' means. He's a bridge builder."

This is a papacy that represents bridge-building to an extraordinary degree, at a time of extraordinary need. His election was achieved by an apparent coalescence of conservative, moderate, and progressive cardinals. He stands as a bridge between North and South America, and between the Latin American experience that had begun with Pope Francis and Rome, the heart of the Church.

Above all, he is a builder of bridges—of continuity and integration—among the pontificates that immediately preceded him, the Second Vatican Council (1962–1965), the Fathers of the Church (particularly the Doctor of the Church St. Augustine of Hippo), and the monumental work of Catholic social teaching that was given its first powerful impetus in the pontificate and the person of Pope Leo XIII (r. 1878–1903) in his 1891 encyclical *Rerum novarum*.

We are at the very start of this new pontificate. And yet, with serenity, calm authority, and gentle firmness, Pope Leo XIV has already established himself as pope and successor not only to Popes Francis, Benedict XVI, and St. John Paul II, but to all of his 266 predecessors—starting with Simon Peter, whose tomb rests beneath the baldacchino of the basilica that bears his name.

This biography of our new Holy Father serves as a portrait of the life, formation, and unprecedented journey of Robert Francis Prevost to the papacy. It is a journey of faith, of hope, of service, but most of all love for Christ and His Church. The pontificate of Leo XIV has begun with a prayer for the peace of the risen Christ. In the days after those first words, we have seen a pontiff mindful of the immensity and eternal relevance of Church teaching, which can and must be proposed anew to an increasingly unbelieving world.

LEO XIV:
Portrait of the First American Pope

Introduction:
Destined for Greater Things

*All intelligent men are agreed, and We Ourselves have with pleasure intimated it above, that America seems destined for greater things. Now, it is Our wish that the Catholic Church should not only share in, but help to bring about, this prospective greatness.*²

THESE ARE THE WORDS of Pope Leo XIII, written in January 1895 in the encyclical *Longinqua* (also known as "On Catholicism in the United States"), to the leaders of the Catholic Church in the United States of America. He could not have known, unless by some divine inspiration, that the next pope to share his name would be raised from that nation.

It is an honor many thought would never be accorded to the United States, at least not in the foreseeable future, and at least as long as the nation remained dominant in the world. Bishop Robert Barron has related that the late Cardinal Francis George of Chicago would say that as long as America remained a superpower, it would never have a pope. This is because the Church could not appear to be the tool of a political hegemon.

Whether the elevation of Cardinal Robert Prevost as Pope Leo XIV indicates the decline of American power is, of course, yet to be seen. But what cannot be denied is that, as the Church has bestowed so many blessings on America, now America has bestowed a gift on the Church.

This is a beautiful, but also ironic fulfillment of the words of the previous Leo:

> For even as your cities, in the course of one century, have made a marvellous increase in wealth and power, so do we behold the Church, from scant and slender beginnings, grown with rapidity to be great and exceedingly flourishing. Now if, on the one hand, the increased riches and resources of your cities are justly attributed to the talents and active industry of the American people, on the other hand, the prosperous condition of Catholicity must be ascribed, first indeed, to the virtue, the ability, and the prudence of the bishops and clergy; but in no slight measure also, to the faith and generosity of the Catholic laity.[3]

But at some point between Leo XIII and Leo XIV, the fortunes of America and the American Church diverged. The nation remained a dominant world power—and, after the collapse of the Soviet Union, the single undisputed world power—but Catholic culture in America, especially in the Northeast and Pope Leo XIV's beloved Midwest, has struggled to keep up.

As we will see, nearly all the Catholic institutions that nurtured Robert Prevost's early life, propelling him to accept God's call to the priesthood, no longer exist or are seemingly in irremediable decline.

The Catholic share of the U.S. population, after increasing for the first half of the twentieth century, has remained hovering around 20 percent for years — about where it was in Leo XIII's time. Far more importantly, however, the percentage of the fifty-three million self-identified Catholics who attend Mass at least weekly has collapsed, according to Pew Research, to 24 percent. And this is an actual increase as Catholics slowly return to regular Mass attendance at pre-COVID pandemic levels.

Moreover, America's civic and cultural life appear to be catching up with Catholic decline. The nation's self-confidence, from trust in its institutions to belief in its purpose and goodness, is at a historic low. Some suspect that Cardinal George may have been right after all: an American pope means the decline of American power.

If Leo XIII were here, he would offer a diagnosis that this crisis of confidence and purpose is directly related to the American Church's crisis of confidence and purpose. He wrote to American Catholics in 1895:

> For without morality the State cannot endure — a truth which that illustrious citizen of yours [George Washington], whom We have just mentioned, with a keenness of insight worthy of his genius and statesmanship perceived and proclaimed. But the best and strongest support of morality is religion.... Now what is the Church other than a legitimate society, founded by the will and ordinance of Jesus Christ for the preservation of morality and the defence of religion?[4]

Leo XIII went on to write that the Church's "fountain of blessings" pours out "in the order of temporal things." In other words, the graces of Christ mediated by the Church don't just support our spiritual lives and our journey to Heaven. They are also indispensable supports for happiness in this life, including political peace and civic resilience.

And so the timing could not be more fitting for a new Leo to come onto the scene. Now, just as in the time of Leo XIII, the world is undergoing tremendous political, economic, and above all technological upheaval. And America is at the forefront.

What will a pope born in the United States offer today's world? We do not yet know. But we can read the signs of the times — to quote a favorite phrase of the Second Vatican Council — and attempt to discern what God might have in store for the Church and the world in delivering an American, Leo XIV, to be our Holy Father.

Beyond the Dictatorship of Relativism

The world is changing at breakneck speed. The international order that has prevailed since the end of the Second World War is transitioning to something new and different. What that will be, and how destabilizing the transition will be, we do not yet know, but Pope Francis was truly insightful when he declared that we are not living in an era of change but a change of era.

A technological revolution, in the form of artificial intelligence, is reshaping politics and the economy at least as much as the internal combustion engine did. But AI's effects may be even more profound: It is radically changing our relationships with knowledge, with creativity, with work, with each other, and with ourselves.

What does it mean to be human? Are human beings special in any meaningful way? Is it worth it to create more people? Is human civilization itself worth preserving? What about human creativity, human friendships, human work? These are questions that have been raised, in some form, throughout the modern and postmodern age, but AI raises the stakes to an existential level: it offers the possibility of truly and finally saying no to humankind.

This follows on the heels of smartphones and social media, which have made people much more connected in the abstract, and yet much more fractured and more anxious, less trusting and less happy. The mass media, as Leo XIV has observed, constantly offers alternatives to Catholic truth, and makes them seem attractive or, worse, inevitable. Now, this media has near-constant access to almost every person, including children.

And all this is happening as the Catholic Church is experiencing more division than she has in generations, if not centuries. The trends of political polarization that have swept the world have not bypassed the Church. Discussions over the Church's place in and posture toward the modern world, which have been going on for generations, have recently become more urgent and less trusting — both of fellow Catholics and of the institutional Church — with some people going as far as to wonder if the risk of schism or total institutional collapse might be imminent.

Meanwhile, the concerns that preoccupied the late Pope Benedict XVI, such as what he called in 2005 the "dictatorship of relativism," are today no longer hypothetical. The dominant culture has moved beyond proposing that all truths are equal, or that we cannot know the truth: new ideologies instead propose that truths long taken for granted, such as the definition of the sexes or the centrality of the nuclear family to society, are simply wrong. And they propose new truths to replace them, imposed by a cancel culture and draconian monitoring of speech, thought, and deed.

So the Church is faced with a new reality: emergent technologies and ideologies that can and will reshape the world. In fact, they are reshaping the world at this very moment and at a pace that surpasses every other technological and intellectual revolution of the past.

We are brought, then, to another majestic document of Leo XIII. Four years before writing to American Catholics, the great pontiff reflected profoundly on the Church's response to the shattering change wrought by the Industrial Revolution. The document laid the foundations of Catholic social teaching: *Rerum novarum*. Or, fittingly, "Of new things."

New Things

On only the second full day of his papacy, Leo XIV addressed the College of Cardinals that had just elected him pope, and he explained his regnal name:

> There are different reasons for this, but mainly because Pope Leo XIII in his historic encyclical *Rerum Novarum* addressed the social question in

the context of the first great industrial revolution. In our own day, the Church offers to everyone the treasury of her social teaching in response to another industrial revolution and to developments in the field of artificial intelligence that pose new challenges for the defence of human dignity, justice and labour.[5]

The message is clear: In response to the "new things" of our age, the world needs a renewal of Catholic witness. And the Church needs a renewal of her social teaching.

Put simply, Catholic social teaching is the application of the Church's deposit of teachings on faith and morals to the spheres of politics, society, and economics. In many respects, the applications in particular instances allow for a great deal of leeway: "prudential judgments" that are nevertheless informed by indispensable Catholic principles. These foundational principles, such as maintaining and defending the dignity of the human person and pursuit of the common good, hold across all times and places.

For instance, the principle of distributive justice holds that a society's material resources should be distributed such that no person has less than he or she needs to live decently — including raising a family of whatever size God ordains. At the same time, every person has an obligation to contribute to society through work — including work in the domestic sphere — to the extent possible.

The key principle of subsidiarity holds that social problems should be addressed at the appropriate level of authority, and generally at the lowest level prudent. This holds open space for the freedom and independence of families and local communities to order their lives as they see fit. And the principle of solidarity, which bore wonderful fruit in Poland when its people were oppressed by the communist Soviet Union, holds that we must recognize our interdependence, and therefore remain focused on the common good more than our own good.

The common good was later defined in *Gaudium et spes*, the Second Vatican Council's document on the Church in the modern world, as "the sum of those conditions of social life which allow social groups and their individual members relatively thorough and ready access to their own fulfillment."[6] That language may appear at first reading to be rather abstruse. Another way to think about it is that the goods that are truly common are those that can be shared without being diminished. When more people share in civil peace, for instance, that peace is not consumed. Just the opposite: the more people share in peace, the greater that peace spreads and finds expression.

Leo XIII did not define all of these ideas in *Rerum novarum*, but he laid the foundation on which future pontiffs clarified, renewed, and augmented his teaching in response to the political and economic realities of their time. That is why every pope since Leo XIII authored what are termed "social encyclicals." They include Pope Pius XI in *Quadragesimo anno* (1931), Pope St. John XXIII in *Pacem in terris* (1963), Pope St. Paul VI in *Populorum progressio* (1967), Pope St. John Paul II in *Centesimus annus* (1991), Pope Benedict XVI in

Caritas in veritate (2009), and Pope Francis in *Laudato si'* (2015) and *Fratelli tutti* (2020).

Now, Pope Leo XIV is clearly indicating that the time has come to renew and expand Catholic social teaching once again, today in response to the digital and AI revolutions.

Authentic expressions of the Church's social teaching always have this essential trait: they do not conform with any existing secular ideology. In *Rerum novarum*, Leo XIII excoriated the industrialists who exploited factory workers and sharply criticized a laissez-faire economy that permits — and even encourages and rewards — this exploitation. But he also strongly defended private property and condemned those ideologies, such as socialism, which denied the importance of property.

A renewal of Catholic social teaching for the contemporary world will not flatter any one political figure or movement, nor will it be describable with any single adjective. It won't be "conservative" or "progressive," though it almost certainly will contain elements of conservatism — concern about the pace of change and reliance on social traditions — and progressivism — a commitment to robust reforms to alleviate unjust social conditions.

Some commentators have already tried to portray Leo XIV as hostile to U.S. President Donald Trump and Vice President J. D. Vance on the basis of a few social media posts in recent years and months. This is a very easy way to misunderstand the Holy Father and the Church's social teaching as a whole. A renewal of Catholic social teaching will rankle every political leader and movement. Its insistence on the dignity of human life from conception to natural death, for instance, will place it at odds with the political left on some matters, the political right on other matters, and technological antihumanists—who imagine the replacement of human beings with artificial intelligence—on just about everything.

But what will guide this new Leo's response to the contemporary world? What will distinguish his approach to Catholic social teaching from his predecessors'? The answer is likely in the theological tradition to which he has dedicated his life: that of St. Augustine.

One in One

As we will see, Leo XIV has been affiliated with the Augustinian Order, and devoted to St. Augustine, since his freshman year of high school. The great Doctor of the Church informs everything the new pope believes about Christ, His Church, and their relationship with the world.

This can be seen in a particular way in Leo's episcopal motto, which is taken from an obscure sermon of St. Augustine on Psalm 127: *In illo uno unum*, which translates as "In the One [Christ], we are one." Here we see the new pope's enduring emphasis on Christian unity—but that unity is founded in the Divine Person of Jesus Christ.

In other words, the Church's response to the crises of the world, and division within itself, is a renewed emphasis on Christian unity *in and through Jesus Christ*. This means that unity isn't about everyone moving in lockstep or adopting all the same practices or holding all the same political views: it is about charity—that is, love of God.

This is fundamental to Augustinian theology, and it is fundamental to Leo XIV's ministry.

Tellingly, in the same passage from which Leo excerpted his motto, St. Augustine also observes: *Multi homines sunt, et unus homo est; multi enim Christiani, et unus Christus.* "There are many men, and yet One Man; for there are many Christians, and One Christ." In other words, our unity in Christ does not destroy our diversity or our individuality. Rather, it enhances them.

There's no evidence St. Augustine ever wrote or said this famous quote attributed to him: "In essentials, unity; in non-essentials, diversity; in all things, charity." But the passage from which Leo XIV gathered his episcopal motto comes very close to describing this idea.

In his early homilies and remarks, Leo XIV has consistently focused his listeners on the Person of Christ. On the loggia above St. Peter's Square, he addressed the faithful not just with a generic wish of peace, but specifically in "the peace of the risen Christ." And in his first public homily, Leo considered that enduring question posed by Christ to Leo's own predecessor, Peter: "Who do you say that I am?"

And Leo's response was to emphasize Christ's Divine Person, the One in whom we are one. Christ was not "a kind of charismatic leader or superman," as many suppose today. Yet he went farther, asserting that many Christians, too, think of Jesus like this — and as a result they live "in a state of practical atheism."[7]

Because if Jesus is not "the Christ, the Son of the living God," as the first Peter answered, then what's the point? If

Christ is just a special man, there is no basis for Christian unity, or unity at all. Therefore there is no basis for solidarity and justice and peace. There is only power and confusion and chaos.

And, Leo XIV is telling us, this is not speculation. Just look around: it's reality.

PART 1

CHICAGO: CITY OF THE BIG SHOULDERS

CHAPTER 1

An American Upbringing

THE POET CARL SANDBERG famously called Chicago "the city of the big shoulders." Those shoulders have now lifted up a Vicar of Christ.

Robert Francis Prevost was born on September 14, 1955, at Mercy Hospital in the Bronzeville neighborhood of the South Side of Chicago. Like so many other hospitals of the same name across America, this one was founded in the nineteenth century by the Sisters of Mercy.

Fifty-eight years prior, Ven. Augustus Tolton died in the same hospital where Leo XIV was born. Fr. Tolton was the first black American Catholic priest, born into slavery in Missouri in 1854. He and his family escaped in 1863 to Illinois, where he demonstrated remarkable intelligence and holiness, resulting in his being sent to the Pontifical Urban University in Rome. He was ordained there in 1886 and celebrated his first Mass in St. Peter's Basilica.

Nearly a century and a half later, Robert Prevost would celebrate Mass in that same Mother Church of Rome, as the 266th successor of St. Peter. And that pontiff, who has family roots in black American Catholicism, would be devoted to the same saint for whom Fr. Tolton was named: St. Augustine. There are no coincidences in God's providence.

Robert was the third of three boys (with older brothers John Joseph Prevost and Louis Martin Prevost) born to Mildred and Louis Prevost, who settled in Dolton, Illinois—a suburb just beyond the southern border of the city of Chicago, closer to Indiana than to the Loop. This was a modest red-brick Cape Cod–style home—212 E 141st Place—in a modest neighborhood, originally built to house workers for this heavily industrialized part of the region, which was and is a major railroading hub: you can't go more than a few blocks without crossing tracks.

At the time of Leo's election, the home happened to be on the market, listed at $199,900 for about 1,200 square feet of living space. The house doesn't even look that big, however, and a previous listing marketed it as only 750 square feet. It's the kind of small but solid home that countless American boys and girls grew up in, probably bouncing off the walls a little bit—especially with three Prevost boys close in age—but also enjoying the close-knit surrounding neighborhood.

That neighborhood was deeply Catholic: the kind of place where going to Mass went without saying, and where the local parish was the center of community life not just on Sunday but every day of the week. The Prevost family could have easily walked the half mile from their Dolton home across the city line (and a few railroad tracks) into the Riverdale section of Chicago, where St. Mary of the Assumption Church was located.

The Church in a Church

The story of St. Mary of the Assumption parish is the story of the Catholic Church in America, especially in older cities like Chicago.

In the 1880s, Chicago was pushing further and further south. From roughly 103rd to 115th Streets, the Pullman Company constructed a company town for its railcar factory workers. But it wasn't enough. The city kept growing, eventually reaching and crossing the Little Calumet River, forming a neighborhood called Riverdale.

German American families in Riverdale petitioned the archdiocese for a parish of their own, and in 1886 the Irish-born archbishop Patrick Feehan approved the request. The next year, the church was completed. As with so many similar churches in burgeoning cities from Providence to Pittsburgh, it was the faith, the funds, and the labor of working-class families that built a home for Jesus in their midst.

The small parish was originally served by Benedictines, according to a history of the Church in Chicago written in 1920, until the archdiocese assumed responsibility after the turn of the century. As Chicago and its suburbs continued to expand, in 1917 the parish completed a stately combined church-and-school building that stands, though abandoned, to this day. It is tucked in a corner of the city of Chicago: the city line is merely a few feet to the south and to the west.

The parish school was originally served by religious sisters called the Poor Handmaids of Jesus Christ. Later, the Sisters of Christian Charity staffed the school. This, too, is a perfect microcosm of the American Church of that era: an exemplary

Catholic school created by the faithful and staffed by nuns committed to education.

And Chicago continued to grow. Although Dolton and far-south Chicago generally have never ceased to be heavily industrialized, during the wave of suburbanization that followed the Second World War, they also became bedroom communities. St. Mary of the Assumption's building was, once again, obsolete, and so the parish constructed a standalone church facing S Leyden Avenue and E 138th Street. That church was completed in 1957, two years after Robert Prevost, the future Pope Leo XIV, was born.

Like so many Catholic boys in Dolton and Riverdale and across the country, Robert served at the altar and sang in the choir. But this wasn't some kind of resented parental imposition: from an early age, the youngest brother showed a keen interest in his family's Faith and in the priesthood. He was reverent at church and played Mass at home, demonstrating a love for the liturgy that has clearly continued to today.

That he would become a priest, in fact, was obvious to his brothers. "Nobody else in our 'hood played priest, but Robert did. And our parents always supported his wishes in that area," Louis told *People* magazine. He added in an interview with CBS News, "We knew as a family from a very young age, there was something special about Rob.... While I was out playing boy games, you know, whether it was baseball, cops and robbers, tag, flashlight, whatever kid games. Rob used to like to play priest." While playing priest, young Robert would pretend to say Mass with Necco wafers on an ironing board. The neighbors were also convinced he would become a priest and even joked that "Bob" would one day become pope. But he was also an active young man who played baseball and who was a fan — a lifelong one as it turned out — of the Chicago White Sox.

St. Mary of the Assumption parish, however, would not live to see its son's remarkable future. Continued suburban sprawl thinned out the flock, changing the social conditions that made tight-knit Catholic communities possible. And Catholic practice itself thinned out in an increasingly materialistic and secular world.

Young Robert also would have experienced the changes of the Second Vatican Council (1962 to 1965) firsthand, with abrupt changes to liturgical practices and the aesthetics of his parish. However, because the Mass of Pope St. Paul VI — today known at the *novus ordo* or the ordinary form of the Mass — was only promulgated in 1969, he would not have experienced it in elementary school. Rather, it coincided with his entering a high-school minor seminary.

Less than two decades after the future Pope Leo graduated from elementary school, his home parish was in decline. It would later be merged with several other parishes, and in 2011 the last Mass was celebrated at the parish that nurtured Robert Prevost's precocious faith. Today, the 1957 church stands abandoned on an overgrown lot.

Melting Pot

But in the 1950s and 1960s, Louis and Mildred Prevost raised their three boys in a community where the Catholic Church and the parish church were the center of life. The idea that St.

Mary of the Assumption might one day stand empty among weeds would have seemed absurd.

The Prevost family is itself a microcosm of America. The family has French, Spanish, Italian, and black Creole roots. From the very beginning, therefore, Leo was both deeply American and deeply international. For that era, the Prevost home also seemed to be strikingly ordinary in its robust Catholicism.

Louis Marius Prevost was born in Chicago in 1920 to parents Salvatore Giovanni Gaetano Riggitano (later John Riggitano Prevost), a Sicilian, and Suzanne Fontaine, who was born in the northern French city of Le Havre. They had two boys, first John Centi and second Louis Marius, and Suzanne became a Third Order Carmelite. In French, the family's name would be pronounced "pray-voh," but in Chicago they went by, and still go by, "pree-vohst."

Louis served in the Navy during the Second World War. According to the Department of Defense, "He was commissioned in November 1943 and became the executive officer of a tank landing ship. He participated in the D-Day landings in Normandy, France, June 6, 1944, as part of Operation Overlord. He also commanded an infantry landing craft, which the Allies used to land infantry soldiers and Marines onto beaches during the war." He was later sent to southern France as part of Operation Anvil-Dragoon in 1944. "Prevost spent 15 months overseas and attained the rank of lieutenant junior grade before the war in Europe finally ended, May 8, 1945."[8]

Exactly eighty years later, his son would be elected pope.

After the war, Louis's calling—like his wife's—would be as an educator. He served in leadership roles in multiple public schools in Chicago's South Side, as well as Mount Carmel Elementary School in the suburb Chicago Heights and was active in the local Altar and Rose Society as well as the Confraternity of Christian Doctrine—this is, he taught CCD. He died in 1997 as a resident of Homewood, a few suburbs south of the family's original home in Dolton.

Louis married the former Mildred Agnes Martínez on January 25, 1949. Mildred was the daughter of Joseph Martínez and Louise Baquié. Joseph was born on the island of Hispaniola—some documents indicate Haiti, others the Dominican Republic—while Louise was black Creole, an amalgam of Louisiana French, Caribbean (black and Hispanic), and African-American descendants of slaves.

Mildred was born Chicago in 1911 but had roots in the Seventh Ward of New Orleans, an area just north of the French Quarter that the *New York Times* described as "traditionally Catholic and a melting pot of people with African, Caribbean and European roots."[9] The Martínez family was faithfully Catholic—two of Mildred's sisters became nuns. After graduating from Immaculata High School in 1929, Mildred attended DePaul University, a Vincentian college in Chicago, where she earned a degree in library science, a still relatively rare feat for women in that era.

Mildred worked as a librarian at nearby Mendel High School while spending countless hours at St. Mary of the Assumption—attending daily Mass, volunteering for committees, sewing vestments, raising money, and singing in the choir. Indeed, the *Times* has reported that Mildred — or Millie, as her friends called her — was "an accomplished singer" who could, and would regularly, perform Schubert's famous setting of the "Ave Maria."[10]

The Prevost family, and in a particular way Mildred, was clearly one of the "first families" of their parish, who could be counted on to be a steady presence at Mass and to contribute in whatever way was needed for the good of their church and the Church. The home was frequented by priests who enjoyed her cooking and who felt welcome. "She was just one of those people you meet and you feel the presence of God," Bishop Daniel Turley — formerly of Chulucanas, Peru, where Leo served in the eighties — told the *Times*. Mildred died of cancer in 1990.

Augustine on the Lake

In 1885, a man named Dorr Eugene Felt invented one of the earliest calculating machines, called the comptometer. In a way he never could have expected, nearly a century later, the wealth generated by this device would come to serve another man with a mathematical bent: Robert Francis Prevost.

Felt and his wife, Agnes, eventually built a tremendous mansion on land near Lake Michigan outside Holland, Michigan. They completed the project in 1928, but it was hardly used before both Agnes and Dorr died — Agnes only six weeks after moving in, and Dorr about a year and a half later. They left the mansion to their four daughters, who didn't have much interest in it. Eventually they sold it to the

Province of Our Mother of Good Counsel, the Chicago-based province of the Augustinian Order.

The Felt Mansion and the beautiful land around it became the home of the St. Augustine Seminary High School, at first a boarding school (day students were admitted later on) for Catholic boys to receive a secondary education while discerning the priesthood in the Augustinian Order. It was here where the future Leo XIV would begin his high school education in 1969 — the very year Pope St. Paul VI promulgated his reformed Mass.

At St. Augustine, Leo excelled across the board, including leading the school yearbook to second place in a national contest. Here is the full text of a story that appeared under the headline "Robert Prevost is Commended" in the *Holland Evening Sentinel* on October 9, 1972:

> Robert Prevost, a senior at St. Augustine Seminary High School, has been awarded a Letter of Commendation honoring him for his high performance on the 1971 Preliminary Scholastic Aptitude Test/National Merit Scholarship Qualifying Test, according to his principal, the Rev. John Peck, OSA.
>
> He is the son of Mr. and Mrs. Louis M. Prevost of Dolton, Ill.
>
> Provost [sic] has consistently been on the Honor Roll. His activities and offices include editor in chief of the yearbook, National Honor Society, vice president and past secretary of Student Council, past president of Library Club, Mission Club, senator

>to the Student Congress in Lansing, president of the senior class.
>
>He plans to continue his study with the Order of St. Augustine for the Priesthood. He presently intends to major in mathematics or psychology in college.

It ended up being mathematics. Leo continued his Augustinian formation at Villanova University—named for the Augustinian St. Thomas of Villanova, whose relic is set in Leo's pectoral cross—outside Philadelphia. While there, the *New York Post* reports, he and other students founded the university's first pro-life club, said to be the oldest in the country, in the wake of the 1973 *Roe v. Wade* decision.

Leo seems not to have participated in the political and cultural battles that roiled campus, as students protested the Vietnam War and attempted to overturn campus rules they found conservative and restrictive. Though the *Philadelphia Inquirer* does report that Leo had a lighter side: He showed up to a 1976 Halloween party dressed as Groucho Marx.[11]

Throughout his college years, though, it is clear that service to the Church was on his mind. After having graduated from the Augustinian minor seminary, Leo was part of the prenovitiate program at Villanova. There is no evidence, from the age of fourteen onward, that he ever strayed from his chosen path—or rather his calling—to the Augustinian priesthood.

Leo also served the Church by working as a groundskeeper at the St. Denis Church cemetery, a few towns down Philadelphia's wealthy Main Line. Words like "humble" and "humility" are often thrown around too easily; for instance, applied to ostentatious displays of service rather than to quieter, less visible commitments. The words themselves—*humble* and *humility*—both derive from the Latin *humus*, which means "dirt" or "earth." Respecting the immortality of the soul by tending to the land in which these souls earthly remains are buried is, therefore, nearly the very definition of humble.

Indeed, he would have passed the exclusive and world-famous Merion Golf Club on the route between Villanova and St. Denis. But the path of worldly ambition never seems to have appealed to him. Instead, immediately upon graduating, Robert Prevost enrolled in the Augustinian novitiate for the Province of Our Mother of Good Counsel in St. Louis, Missouri.

CHAPTER 2

Witness to Decline

It is fitting that the first pope from the United States, a country where the Church was seeded by missionaries, should be a missionary himself.

It was December, and it was cold, as Jesuit missionary Fr. Jacques Marquette trudged south near the western shore of Lake Michigan. He had promised the Kaskaskia Indians of the Illinois River Valley that he would return to them, but the weather was awful and his health faltering. Fr. Marquette was only thirty-seven years old, but constant missionary activity in the American and Canadian wilderness had taken its toll.

It soon became clear that he and his band of missionaries would not be able to keep their promise — at least until winter was over. And so they built a cabin in the territory of the Illinois Confederation, in between two parallel rivers the French called Des Plaines and Chicagou, the French interpretation of the local Native Americans' name for ramps, a leek-like root vegetable.

This is the first evidence for European settlement in what is now the city of Chicago.

Fr. Marquette eventually made it to the Kaskaskia, but he died on his return journey on the other side of Lake Michigan.

He had never fully recovered from the dysentery that had drained his energy, and his travels only heightened his exhaustion. His remains are, today, in the town he founded on the north shore of the Strait of Mackinac, in the Upper Peninsula of Michigan: St. Ignace, named for St. Ignatius of Loyola, founder of the Jesuits.

Chicago is geographically important because it is the point where the Great Lakes and the Mississippi River system come closest together. With only a few miles' walk, explorers, traders, and missionaries could transport boats overland and continue their journeys, either into the lakes or into the continent's greatest network of rivers.

This led to Chicago's explosive growth. The first Catholic church, according to the *Catholic Encyclopedia*, was built in 1833 on Lake Street: a wood structure of twenty-five by thirty-five feet, costing about four hundred dollars. Only a little more than a decade later, in 1844, Rome raised the Diocese of Chicago, complementing the Diocese of St. Louis, which had been the first across the Appalachians. In 1880, the diocese became an archdiocese under the leadership of Archbishop Patrick Feehan—the same prelate who, in 1886, would approve the creation of St. Mary of the Assumption parish in Riverdale.

This demonstrates the truly incredible growth of Chicago, and its Catholic community. In only about fifty years, the city went from erecting its very first Catholic church in a tiny wood structure to being a major archdiocese, raising parishes in dense developments over fifteen miles from the city center.

A century later, however, the Church would be in retreat. By the end of the twentieth century, the archdiocese was merging and closing parishes in parts of urban and suburban Chicago that had gone from mission territory to hotbeds of Catholic culture just a few generations prior. It is a story that is familiar to Catholics across the Western world, but particularly in trailblazing Catholic cities in the American Northeast and Midwest, such as St. Louis, Boston, and Baltimore.

Pope Leo XIV lived through the transition from growth and exuberance to decline and exhaustion. You can see it in all the places that nurtured his faith.

Decline and Fall

In the mid-1950s, St. Mary of the Assumption Parish in the Riverdale neighborhood of Chicago was growing so fast it commissioned a new, expanded church building to accommodate worshippers and free up space in its school building. One generation later, in the 1980s, it had entered terminal decline.

In 2011, it was closed. In 2025—until May 8, when it became a source of international interest—it had been all but forgotten.

It is a story known to Catholics from all over America, but especially industrial boom towns where Catholic immigrants settled. In Riverdale it started as German Catholics in the 1880s. And by the 1950s suburbanization had brought a new wave of people to Chicago's outskirts.

These were the days when Catholic culture seemed poised to last forever: where big families sent their children to Catholic schools, often walking because the parish was a truly neighborhood institution; where neighborhood establishments served fish on Fridays and closed on feast days; where Catholicism and its habits and practices and beliefs were taken for granted; where the parish was the center of community life, not just for Mass, but for education and socialization and charity.

But it didn't last, not even for one more generation. Robert Prevost was an altar boy and choir member while everything seemed to be fine. By the time he was ordained a priest in 1982, his parish was shrinking, and it would never recover.

The reasons are complicated, and have to do with social, political, economic, geographic, and cultural factors at least as much as ecclesiastical ones. The Second Vatican Council coincided with many of these shifts and interacted with them in complicated ways. For some everyday parishioners, the changes to the experience of the Church, from education to governance to liturgy, were refreshing; for others, they were disappointing and destabilizing.

As Jonathan Liedl writes in the National Catholic Register in a piece titled, "Visiting Pope Leo XIV's Chicago: How the South Side Shaped America's First Pontiff," "Amidst the changing demographics of the area, white ethnic Catholics moved further out into the suburbs. Membership in the massive network of South Side parishes that had been built to sustain the Catholic population began to dwindle, while debts piled up. St. Mary of the Assumption, Pope Leo XIV's childhood parish and a once-bustling epicenter of Catholic activity, now lies gutted and abandoned. A hole is in its roof and graffiti covers the sanctuary walls."[12]

The important point, however, is that in America — and in places like Dolton and Riverdale in particular — it all happened at once, and Pope Leo XIV saw it happen. The

Church's proposition to the world was no longer being taken up, or even taken seriously. Catholic culture dissipated—or remained *only* as culture, with its spiritual core hollowed out. That is, as the Augustinian Leo would put it, with the person of Jesus Christ placed aside, resulting in "a state of practical atheism."

Christ Is the Answer

This decline can also be seen in the fate of Leo's minor seminary, St. Augustine, on the eastern shores of Lake Michigan. The high school, whose purpose was to prepare candidates for more advanced priestly formation while also providing an all-around education, acquired the property on which it was built in 1949. Leo attended from 1969 to 1973. And in 1977 it closed for good.

For the next fourteen years, the Felt Mansion property was used by the Michigan Department of Corrections. Today, it's a park.

Why were middle-school boys no longer considering using high school as a period of discernment, in a seminary-like environment? Perhaps more importantly, why were parents no longer encouraging their sons to consider such an option? Why did the choice that Robert Prevost made—and the encouragement that his parents provided—become so uncommon that so many centers of Catholic life and formation had no choice but to close their doors?

These are the questions the Church has struggled to address, especially in America, for several decades now. And they are the personal experience of Pope Leo XIV.

It's too easy to blame the collapse of these institutions, and the Catholic sensibilities that sustained them, on the Second Vatican Council, or its application, or its reception. Obviously Leo doesn't take this approach. Here are his remarks on the Council in his first address to the College of Cardinals:

> I would like us to renew together today our complete commitment to the path that the universal Church has now followed for decades in the wake of the Second Vatican Council. Pope Francis masterfully and concretely set it forth in the Apostolic Exhortation *Evangelii Gaudium*, from which I would like to highlight several fundamental points: the return to the primacy of Christ in proclamation; the missionary conversion of the entire Christian community; growth in collegiality and synodality; attention to the *sensus fidei* [the sense of the faithful], especially in its most authentic and inclusive forms, such as popular piety; loving care for the least and the rejected; courageous and trusting dialogue with the contemporary world in its various components and realities.
>
> These are evangelical principles that have always inspired and guided the life and activity of God's Family. In these values, the merciful face of the Father has been revealed and continues to be revealed in his incarnate Son, the ultimate hope of all who sincerely seek truth, justice, peace and fraternity.[13]

This is not a radical commitment to change, but a confident assertion that the Church has within her, informed by Vatican

II, the resources necessary to confront her challenges. In a particular way, as he has already done so consistently, Leo turns his attention and ours to the Person of Jesus Christ, the Son of God, without whom there can be no authentic hope or progress.

In 2023, shortly after being made a cardinal by Pope Francis, Leo gave an interview with the Augustinian Order that touched on these issues — and always returned to Christ.

> First of all, our priority cannot be to look for vocations. Our priority has to be to live the good news, to live the Gospel, to share the enthusiasm that can be born in our hearts and in our lives when we truly discover who Jesus Christ is. When we stay walking with Christ, in communion with one another, in that friendship with the Lord and understanding how great it is to have received that gift, vocations come.[14]

In other words, the challenge is not technical or strategic: It's not that the Church needs to use social media better, or to engage consultants about how to create programs that encourage young men and women to pursue religious vocations. It's the witness of living a life in love with Christ, which in turn reflects the love of Christ to others, that draws people to Him. And that's what generates an interest in following God's call to walk with Him in a special way as a priest or religious.

All In, or All Out

In the American Catholic upbringing of Pope Leo XIV, we see the story of the Church in so much of America in microcosm.

We see early years of exuberance and confidence, when the allure of secularism and materialism were clear but collapse seemed unimaginable. Then follows a period of transition, when decline had already begun—such as the 1977 closure of the St. Augustine minor seminary—and many thought the answer was to become more like the world, instead of more distinct from it.

And then the final collapse of the spiritual infrastructure that had sustained so many people and communities for so long.

This isn't to say that the Church is in dire straits in the same way all over America. The Catholic share of the population has remained somewhat stable largely due to immigration from Catholic cultures, especially from Latin America. In parts of the country where these communities are growing strongly—many of which are places that did not experience the boom-and-bust of the Northeast and the Midwest—parishes are growing and bursting at the seams.

And yet we have to wonder: Will these undergo the same process as St. Mary of the Assumption in Chicago? After this period of exuberance, will they also begin to stagnate and eventually decline, as migration patterns change and generational attrition kicks in? The early data is discouraging: second-generation Catholic immigrants in America don't go to Mass as frequently as their parents did. Will parishes planted in suburban Dallas, for instance, seem obsolete in just a few decades?

This is why the questions posed by Leo's Chicago Catholic upbringing aren't just forensic: they're urgent for discerning how the Church can respond to the present moment, in the pope's country of birth and around the world. In that same Augustinian interview, here's how then-Cardinal Prevost described the challenge:

> The mission of the Church has been the same for 2000 years, when Jesus Christ said: "Go therefore and make disciples of all nations, baptising them in the name of the Father and of the Son and of the Holy Spirit, teaching them to observe all that I have commanded you" (Mt 28:19). We have to announce the good news of the Kingdom of God at the same time that we understand what the church is in its universal reality.... There are many different cultures, many different languages, many different circumstances around the world where the church responds. So when we list our priorities and weigh up the challenges before us we have to be aware that the urgencies of Italy, Spain, the United States, Peru or China, for example, are almost certainly not the same except in one thing: the underlying challenge that Christ left to us to preach the Gospel and that this is the same everywhere.

This is the same everywhere. Here we return once again to Leo's Augustinian motto: *In illo unum uno.* In the One, we are one. Only in encountering Jesus Christ—not the charismatic human leader but the Son of God—can there be a sense of common purpose, as the Body of Christ links arms on the journey to Heaven.

This, in the final analysis, is what is missing when a Catholic community and a Catholic culture dissipates: the conviction that we *are* one in Christ, and therefore we must put aside other priorities in order to toil together, each in the manner and to the degree proper to him or her, in the vineyard of the Lord. If we want human respect or human security or human riches more than we want to be with Jesus, then we will not hold together. And those things we hold dear—our parishes, our schools, our communities—will fall apart, *because we decided other things were more important.*

The city of Chicago was, in a sense, founded by those who decided nothing was more important than Christ, and in particular bringing Christ to those who did not yet know Him. The city's Catholic culture fell apart, Leo would rightly say, once people lost that zeal for Jesus, and therefore ended up losing each other.

This is a deeply Augustinian insight. And it was through the Augustinian Order that Pope Leo XIV came to full maturity in the Church.

CHAPTER 3

Son of Augustine

ON THE CHURCH KNOWN today as Olde St. Augustine's in Philadelphia are carved these defiant words: "FOUNDED 1798. DESTROYED 1844. REBUILT 1847. CONSECRATED 1848."

It was a spring day in Philadelphia, 181 years to the day before Pope Leo XIV's election, and the crowd was restless. Five days prior, a rowdy meeting of nativists, who were opposed to the growth of immigrant communities in the city, had been disrupted by Irish Catholic demonstrators. Then on May 6, nativists and Irish immigrants brawled in the streets all over the city.

Although the American nativists, who would eventually form the Know Nothing Party, were vexed by immigration generally, they were *particularly* vexed by Irish Catholics, and *especially* vexed by one man in particular: the pope. Throughout the violence of May 1844, the nativists desperately warned the people of Philadelphia of a plot by the pope to take over America, distributing leaflets describing "the bloody hand of the pope."

It had begun over, of all things, translations of the Holy Bible. In Philadelphia's public schools at the time, only the King James Version was permitted for reading and instruction.

But by 1842, the Catholic diocese had grown so large and so strong that Irish-born Bishop Francis Kenrick, bishop from 1842–1851, began to raise objections: Why couldn't Catholic students use the Church's approved Douay-Rheims translation for their studies, rather than having a Protestant translation imposed on them?

When a Catholic elected representative suggested pausing Scripture readings in school while the debate transpired, the situation began to boil over. And by May 8, the nativists had several Catholic buildings in their sights and came prepared. First was St. Michael's, a parish that exists to this day (in a rebuilt form) at the corner of Jefferson and Second Streets in what is now called Olde Kensington. Then it was the seminary of the Sisters of Charity, just two blocks away, which is now part of a business district.

The mob had to migrate about one mile south to find its next target: St. Augustine's Church, near Center City—the first parish of the Augustinian Order in the United States. City-paid armed guards, along with the mayor himself, were waiting. But they couldn't hold off the rioters, who pelted the defenders (including the mayor) with rocks and burned the church to the ground.

Of course, for the nativists, what would occur 181 years later would have been their worst nightmare: a pope, and specifically an Augustinian pope, from the United States.

Augustinian Forever

Pope Leo XIV has dedicated himself to the Augustinian Order, and to Augustinian spirituality, for the last fifty-five years of his life. It is why when he introduced himself on the loggia of St. Peter's Basilica minutes after his election, he declared: "I am a son of St. Augustine, an Augustinian."

These words echoed many other statements over the years, including in 2024 when then-Cardinal Prevost was back in Illinois and spoke at St. Jude Catholic Church in Illinois. He began his presentation by saying, "I'm an Augustinian.... I have personally a great debt to the Order of Saint Augustine, to St. Augustine himself, [his] philosophy, theology, thought, humanity; that great love of Augustine for God's Word, that infinite searching for truth, for himself, and for God in himself; and for everything that Augustine taught in terms of communion and community that marked my life."[15]

The Augustinian Order unquestionably has been a part of Pope Leo's life since his childhood. There were influences throughout his formative years, including the Augustinian priests who were a fixture in South Chicago, and it is said that the boy's zeal was so clear that various religious orders in the area attempted to recruit him. But for Leo, it was always Augustine.

Having answered the call to the priesthood and to the Augustinians, after his Augustinian high school and college educations, Robert Prevost immediately enrolled in the novitiate for the midwestern province of the Order of St. Augustine, named for the wonderful Augustinian devotion to Our Lady of Good Counsel. This took the twenty-one-year-old to St. Louis and the stately Immaculate Conception Church, a Gothic masterpiece that could pass for a cathedral (it was built by the same firm that built the Cathedral Basilica of St. Louis). But, like so many of the Catholic institutions that nurtured Leo's faith, it has now fallen into disuse.

Robert Prevost spent one year in St. Louis, and was remembered by parishioners as prayerful, kind, and contemplative. "This guy was a rock star," one friend from that time told the *St. Louis Post-Dispatch*. "You could tell even then he was destined to be great." And yet: "He's an American kid like all of us. There were no airs about him."[16]

One year and one day after entering the novitiate, on September 2, 1978, Robert Prevost made his first vows to the Lord as a member of the Augustinian Order at the province's main church, St. Rita of Cascia, in his hometown of Chicago. Two years later he made his solemn vows. During this time, he earned his master of divinity degree at the Catholic Theological Union in the Hyde Park neighborhood of Chicago's South Side, while also teaching physics and mathematics at St. Rita of Cascia High School, putting to use his degree in mathematics from Villanova. On August 29, 1981, he made his solemn vows.

After showing his intellectual potential, the Order sent Robert Prevost to Rome to further his studies at the Pontifical University of St. Thomas Aquinas, also known as the Angelicum for St. Thomas's nickname of the "Angelic Doctor." The Order wanted him to study canon law under the Dominicans. He earned first a licentiate in canon law (J.C.L.) and then was allowed to proceed to the doctorate.

He completed and then defended his dissertation for the doctorate in canon law (J.C.D.) in 1987. It was titled, "The Office and Authority of the Local Prior in the Order of Saint

Augustine." It looked especially at the role of the local prior within the Augustinian Order, revealing a keen interest in both community life and good governance.

He was ordained a priest in Rome at the Augustinian College of St. Monica on June 19, 1982, by Archbishop Jean Jadot, the former Holy See apostolic delegate to the United States and then pro-president of the Secretariat for Non-Christians, which later became the Pontifical Council for Interreligious Dialogue and then the Dicastery for Interreligious Dialogue.

Three years later—having completed his licentiate and started on the doctorate—he began his first missionary assignment in northern Peru.

In another sign of the high regard the Order's leaders had for him, Robert Prevost returned to Chicago in 1987, at the age of only thirty-one, to serve as the vocations and mission director for the province. Then, after a decade of service in Peru, he was elected as prior provincial in 1998, a role he held for three years before being elevated once again—this time to the prior general of the worldwide Order of St. Augustine.

Rule of Life

The Order of St. Augustine traces its roots to the great saint and Doctor of the Church himself, the fifth-century bishop of Hippo and one of the greatest writers and thinkers to ever live. Whether Augustine himself *founded* the order by holding to a particular rule of life with his companions is contested. What is clear is that in the thirteenth century, several eremitical groups—that is, hermits—were active in what is today northern Italy, and their way of life was modeled on the Rule of St. Augustine. The Rule emphasizes unity in Christ:

> Before all else, beloved, love God and then your neighbor, for these are the chief commandments given to us. (1)
>
> The main purpose for your having come together is to live harmoniously in your house, intent upon God, with one heart and one soul. (3)
>
> Let all of you then live together in oneness of mind and heart, mutually honoring in yourselves the God whose temples you have become. (9)
>
> There should be nothing about your behavior to attract attention. Besides, you should not seek to please by your apparel, but by a good life. Whenever you go out, walk together, and when you reach your destination, stay together. In your walking, standing, and every movement, let nothing occur to give offense to anyone who sees you, but only what becomes your holy state of life. (19–21)

The groups of hermits—to be clear, eremitical monasticism does not mean living entirely isolated, but rather emphasizing individual seclusion and still sharing aspects of a common life—were largely made up of lay people who were inspired to follow Augustine's rule. They were motivated in part by the mendicant movement of the time, embodied by the Franciscans and Dominicans, who sought to bring the great traditions of community life into the world, with a focus especially on itinerant preaching and study. Each of the little groups of

Augustinian-inspired eremites, however, was living in its own way, raising questions of organization and authority.

Over the course of the thirteenth century, multiple popes organized these small groups into a single order, which was known as the *Ordo eremitarum sancti Augustini*, or Order of Hermits of Saint Augustine. Particular credit, however, goes to Pope Innocent IV at the end of 1243, when he issued the bull *Incumbit nobis* that called on the hermits to embrace "the Rule and way of life of the Blessed Augustine." (The word "hermits" was only removed in 1968, a decade before Robert Prevost entered the novitiate.) In the sixteenth century, Pope St. Pius V officially placed the Augustinians among the other mendicant orders.

By this time — in fact, as early as the 1300s — the Augustinians had also become known for their keen interest in missionary work. During the Age of Exploration, many of the most famous wayfarers and conquerors, including Vasco da Gama and Hernán Cortés, were either joined or followed by Augustinian missionaries. This mission work was motivated in a particular way by the Augustinian emphasis on education and human unity in and through Jesus Christ.

Five Relics and One Pectoral Cross

It is impossible to understand Pope Leo XIV without understanding his Augustinian spirituality. And one small but significant window into what that means in practice is to consider in detail a gift given by the Augustinian Order to then Cardinal Prevost at the time of his creation as a cardinal by Pope Francis in 2023: a gold pectoral cross with five relics. A pectoral cross is typically worn by bishops, abbots, archbishops, and cardinals signifying both their authority and the closeness of Christ Crucified to their hearts.

In this case, the gift from the Augustinians contained five relics of five saints closely connected to the Augustinians. Pope Leo XIV wore that pectoral cross on the very day of his election when he stood on the loggia of St. Peter's Basilica. They are: St. Augustine, St. Monica, St. Thomas of Villanova, Bl. Anselmo Polanco, and Ven. Joseph Bartholomew Menochio.

✠ St. Augustine

The man himself. St. Augustine was born in 354 in what is today Algeria. He related the story of his life and dramatic conversion in the *Confessions*, the first autobiography in Western literature. It begins with some of the most famous devotional lines ever written:

> Great art Thou, O Lord, and greatly to be praised; great is Thy power, and of Thy wisdom there is no end.... Thou movest us to delight in praising Thee; for Thou hast formed us for Thyself, and our hearts are restless till they find rest in Thee.

Augustine knew this restlessness all too well. Whereas his mother, later known as St. Monica, was a faithful Christian, as a young man Augustine reveled in sin, from the famously transgressive theft of pears just because he could, to carrying on with a concubine when he knew this was against God's law and was the source of such terrible suffering for his mother.

Augustine eventually put his tremendous talents to work as a teacher of rhetoric, and it was this that brought him in touch with another Doctor of the Church, St. Ambrose, bishop of Milan. This relationship developed into an intellectual and spiritual mentorship, culminating in Augustine's baptism at the age of thirty-two. The deaths of Augustine's mother and son left him alone, and he sold his family's significant possessions, delivering the proceeds to the poor.

His oratorical skills led him to be named — against his own desires — bishop of Hippo Regius, in what is today northeast Algeria. Here, he served his flock while writing and speaking a tremendous number of words to and for the people of God. His thousands of sermons, along with major texts like the *Confessions* and *City of God*, constitute one of the most impressive intellectual outputs in human history and one of the greatest fonts of learning for Christians ever since. He died in 430 at the age of seventy-five as his city was being besieged by the Arian Vandals.

✠ St. Monica

While St. Ambrose's preaching, genius, and holiness drew St. Augustine to the Christian faith, it was his mother's prayers and love in the midst of suffering that did the heavy lifting. She was born in the early 330s and married a pagan man named Patricius. They had three surviving children, but Patricius would not permit them to be baptized. This made his son Augustine's dissipated behavior as a young man all the more painful: she knew that he lacked the grace of God and that his soul was in peril.

And so she prayed and wept every night for her son — but she never despaired of God's goodness and His ability to bring her son home. And that's exactly what happened. She died only a few months after St. Ambrose baptized her wayward son into the Faith she cherished so much. She famously declared, "There was indeed one thing for which I wished to tarry a little in this life, and that was that I might see you a Catholic Christian before I died. My god has answered this more than abundantly" (*Confessions*, Book IX).

✠ St. Thomas of Villanova

While Sts. Augustine and Monica inspired the Augustinians, St. Thomas of Villanova was one. He was born into a modest but generous family in 1488 in central Spain. An eloquent preacher, he joined the Augustinians in 1516 before receiving ordination in 1518. The effectiveness of his speaking was so profound and far-reaching that the Holy Roman Emperor Charles V, who ruled one of the most extensive European empires in history — from Spain to the Netherlands to Austria and the Americas — brought him into the imperial court.

But what most distinguished Thomas of Villanova was not his words, but his actions. He became archbishop of Valencia in 1544, and upon entering the city is said to have been presented with four thousand silver coins. He replied, "The poor need this more than I. What luxuries and comforts can a simple friar like me want?"

His archbishop's palace became a place of pilgrimage for the poor, and he made sure everyone who asked received what they needed. But he also worked to fix the conditions that led to poverty in the first place, writing that "Charity is not just giving, rather removing the need of those who receive charity and liberating them from it when possible." After a decade of spiritual and material service to the people of Valencia, St. Thomas died in 1555.

✠ Bl. Anselmo Polanco

Bl. Anselmo Polanco, bishop of Teruel and Albarracin in east-central Spain, was one of ninety-nine Augustinians to be martyred during the Spanish Civil War. He was born in 1881 in the northern part of the country and joined the Augustinians at a young age. In 1932, he became prior provincial, which involved trips around the world due to the extent of Augustinian missionary activities. Three years later, he was named bishop.

Then in 1936, the brutal Spanish Civil War commenced. The left-wing, communist-supported Republican faction sought to overturn all traditional authorities in the country, including spiritual ones: from kings and landowners to priests and nuns and simply devout laypeople. Republican victories were typically followed by massacres of Catholics in captured towns.

Bl. Anselmo was one of those captured in 1938. He was executed by firing squad just days before the final defeat of the Republican faction, at which point even in the eyes of the fanatical leftists he could have presented no threat. He was beatified by Pope St. John Paul II in 1995.

✠ Ven. Joseph Bartholomew Menochio

Born in Turin in 1741, Ven. Joseph Bartholomew Menochio took his Augustinian vows in 1764 and later participated in a tradition that goes back to the fifteenth century and continues to this day: that an Augustinian serves as papal sacristan. But the early nineteenth century was a dangerous time to serve the Supreme Pontiff so intimately: Napoleon was on the march.

In July 1809, the French emperor ordered his troops to arrest Pope Pius VII and brought him to France as a prisoner. The pontiff spent the next five years in captivity. The Papal States were then subjected to occupation, and the inhabitants and officials of the Papal States were required to take an oath of fidelity to the French emperor. Joseph Bartholomew remained in Rome and, according to Leo's own Midwest Augustinians, "refused to take the oath of fidelity to the Emperor Napoleon, even though he faced great pressure to do so."[17] After the emperor's fall in 1814, Joseph Bartholomew worked to restore Augustinian communities that had been suppressed by Napoleon. He died in 1823.

Union and Communion

In these Augustinian models, which Pope Leo XIV has chosen to keep close to his heart in his pectoral cross, we can see a remarkable diversity of ways of living out Augustinian spirituality, with one very clear through line: absolute reliance on relationship with Jesus Christ and His Church.

It is in and through Jesus that Augustine's intellect came into full flower and his life became one of heroic and extraordinary virtue and holiness; that Monica persevered in her sorrows and ultimately saw her son become a member of God's family; that Thomas became a model of service who didn't just distribute charity but reformed unjust systems; that Anselmo led his flock through a savage persecution and ultimately gave his life without hesitation; and that Joseph Bartholomew remained faithful to the Church despite worldly pressures to abandon her.

Indeed, that points to another thread that connects these saints: perseverance against worldliness. Augustine could have been a comfortable rhetorician; Monica could have just let her son go and enjoy life as an upper class Roman wife; Thomas could have lived luxuriously as a passive and disinterested bishop; Anselmo could have tried to escape or to make a deal with his captors that would have saved his life; and Joseph Bartholomew could have saved himself much trouble by simply pledging himself to Napoleon.

But that's not what holiness is, Leo XIV is telling us. Holiness is in cleaving to Christ and His Church, always, in all things, through all troubles, in all joys, through all sorrows. As author and expert in the Church Fathers Mike Aquilina noted in a reflection for the National Catholic Register on the motto of Pope Leo XIV as pontiff, *In illo uno unum*, "In the One Christ, we are one," a key concept in understanding Augustinian thought "is his notion of the *Totus Christus*—the 'Whole Christ.' With this phrase, he described the spiritual unity of all Christians as members of Christ's body, with Christ himself as their head. For Augustine, it is something more than a metaphor. It is an image that describes the real and sacramental bond of Christians in the Church."[18]

Here's how Pope Leo put the Augustinian calling in an interview shortly after being made a cardinal:

> When I think of St. Augustine, his vision and understanding of what it means to belong to the Church, one of the first things that springs to mind is what he says about how you cannot say you are a follower of Christ without being part of the Church. Christ is part of the Church. He is the head.
>
> So people who think they can follow Christ "in their own way" without being part of the body, are, unfortunately, living a distortion of what is really an authentic experience. St Augustine's teachings touch every part of life, and help us to live in communion.
>
> Unity and communion are essential charisms of the life of the Order and a fundamental part of understanding what the Church is and what it means to be in it.[19]

Augustinian spirituality is grounded first in the search for truth, following in the spiritually stunning journey of Augustine to conversion and Baptism. Augustine expressed this perfectly when he proclaimed, *Fecisti nos ad te, et inquietum est cor nostrum donec resquiescat in Te.* "You have made us for Yourself, O Lord, and our hearts are restless until they rest in You."

Aquilina adds:

> Augustinian spirituality emphasizes the search for God through interiority, prayer, community, and

service. The model for such a life is St. Augustine, who tells the story of conversion in his memoir, *The Confessions*. The narrative is personal but presumes that the desire for God is universally human — glimpsed in earthly desires, but not fulfilled by earthly objects.[20]

In a particular way, Augustinian spirituality emphasizes the primacy of friendship, both as a gift from God and as a great support in growing closer to Him. Here's how Leo put it in that same interview in 2023:

> Different people can greatly enhance our lives. And, to tell the truth, as an Augustinian, having a rich community built on the ability to share with others what happens to us, to be open to others, has been one of the greatest gifts I have been given in this life. The gift of friendship brings us back to Jesus himself. To have the ability to develop authentic friendships in life is beautiful. Without a doubt, friendship is one of the most wonderful gifts that God has given us.[21]

The Augustinian approach is given expression by the symbol of the Order: a flaming heart pierced by an arrow above an open book. The flaming heart is a traditional image for Augustine embodying the love of God and love of neighbor. The heart is also depicted to have been pierced based on Augustine's proclamation of his encounter with the Word of God: *Vulnerasti cor meum verbo tuo* — "You have pierced my heart with Your Word." The book, meanwhile, symbolizes the search for knowledge that is considered a hallmark of the Augustinian tradition. Burning zeal for evangelization and a desire for knowledge: both were part of Pope Leo XIV's years in the Order's missions in Peru.

PART 2

PERU: LAND OF CONTRASTS

CHAPTER 4

Padre Roberto

THE POPE MAY BE the Bishop of Rome, but in his own heart Pope Leo XIV will always be first the bishop of Chiclayo. It was to the faithful of that small city in northern Peru that he dedicated a special greeting, in Spanish, on his first appearance from the loggia of St. Peter's Basilica on the afternoon of May 8, 2025:

> And if you allow me a brief word, a greeting to all and especially to my beloved Diocese of Chiclayo, in Peru, where a faithful people has accompanied its Bishop, shared its faith and given so much, so much, to continue being a faithful Church of Jesus Christ.[22]

In the hours to come, a fight broke out among the people who dedicate themselves to editing and improving Wikipedia, the crowd-sourced online encyclopedia. The question was: Should Leo XIV be referred to as the "first American pope"? While in the United States, the word *American* clearly indicates a person from the United States, *American* can also refer to a person from the Americas more broadly. Using that definition, Jorge Mario Bergoglio — Pope Francis — was the first American pope.

The details of the argument itself are tedious, but the discussion offers a window into Leo's identity. The fact is, as we can tell from his own remarks, Leo XIV considers himself more closely attached to Peru than to the United States. It is in South America where he dedicated his most intense pastoral efforts, and where he has lived for nearly half of his life as a priest of Jesus Christ.

Whether we call Leo the "first American pope" doesn't really matter, in the end. What matters is that his first identity is in Christ and His Church.

But we can say, unquestionably, that Leo XIV is the first *completely* American pope: he is a man of both American continents, whose understanding of the Church and of the human experience of God is informed by both. He may have begun his missionary work as an American in Peru, but he became a Peruvian — both as a matter of citizenship and as a matter of culture and faith and love.

Indeed, other than Jesus Christ Himself, and the Church He founded, it is clearly Peru that is the love of Leo's life.

First Year

The Order of St. Augustine has been active in Peru since the mid-sixteenth century, as part of its missionary activities around the world. It was 1985 when a young Augustinian Fr. Robert Prevost arrived in Chulucanas, a small city tucked in a strip of land between the Andes Mountains and the Sechura Desert of northern Peru.

Fr. Prevost had been a priest for three years at that point, time he had mostly spent studying canon law — that is, the ecclesiastical law of the Catholic Church — at the Angelicum in Rome. Mission work is what he wanted to do, but nothing in Chicago or Rome could have prepared him for Chulucanas.

This part of Peru is generally quite dry — except during El Niño weather patterns, when waves of rain inundated Peru's Pacific coast. Water rushing down the slopes of the Andes washed away thousands of homes. "He was doing everything he could to help because it was an emergency. People's homes were knocked down. There was so much need — he got his hands dirty," recalled Bishop Dan Turley to Kevin Clarke of *America* magazine.[23]

It was a crash course in the realities of missionary work: Although his first responsibility was always the spiritual well-being of the people he served, the slight, skinny young priest also had to become adept in helping with the material necessities of life.

At the time, Chulucanas was only a "territorial prelature" and not yet a diocese with a bishop, though that would come in a few years' time. The territory Leo was responsible for included the main town, with a few tens of thousands of souls, and then innumerable small communities in the Andean foothills, many of whom were members of indigenous communities who spoke indigenous languages. Although Chulucanas was hardly well-off, the hills were where the deep poverty was found.

This was a radically different kind of poverty than what he would have seen in the South Side of Chicago, and a radically different experience of the supernatural. In many of these villages, the Catholic Faith would have still been in competition with traditional spiritual beliefs and practices. Or the Faith would have been combined with those practices into syncretic belief systems.

Leo's first year in Peru was clearly a formative one for him, the first taste of the life he most longed for. But his Order soon called him to work back in Chicago—including as missions director, demonstrating not just the passion but the expertise and competence he had shown and developed. After finalizing his doctorate at the Angelicum in 1987, it was back to Peru—and this time it became his home.

A Divided Country

Peru can be roughly split into three geographical regions: the desert coast, where most of its citizens live (Lima is the driest capital city in the world); the Andes highlands, home to spectacular heritage sites like Machu Picchu and inhabited to this day by indigenous Peruvians; and the impossibly dense Amazon rainforest, which covers most of the country's land area. In fact, Peru contains more of the Amazon than any other country, besides Brazil.

Leo's ministry would have taken him to all three, but he mostly straddled the coast and the mountains in northern Peru. Here, the dry coast extends inland as far as sixty miles, forming the extremely arid Sechura Desert. The natural color of the landscape here is brown—it almost feels like a sepia-tone photograph—except where irrigation has made agriculture possible.

The brown hills to the north and east of the coastal settlements rise slowly and then suddenly. In these majestic plateaus and flood-prone valleys, traditional ways of life persist, such as ranching and subsistence farming. Poor but picturesque churches dot the landscape, but for many people it's a many-mile trip along treacherous mountain roads to get to Mass. Horses and mules remain important modes of transportation.

The sharp contrast between metropolitan Peru and what Peruvians call Peru *profundo*, or "deep Peru," as well as between the traditional landed gentry and the working and peasant classes, has led to serious political conflict over the centuries. The time Leo spent as a missionary in Peru was one of the most troubled in its history.

From 1980 to 2000, the country suffered through a low-level civil war between Marxist revolutionaries—most notoriously the Shining Path—and successive government regimes. The Shining Path followed a unique brand of Marxist thought associated with its founder, Abimael Guzmán, which emphasized the necessity of violence to achieve total victory against capitalism and the bourgeois classes—including the authority represented by the Catholic Church.

The Shining Path saw itself as *the* vanguard of world communism. After toppling the Peruvian regime, the movement theorized, it would spread its particularly savage version of Marxism-Leninism-Maoism around the world. That also meant exterminating other communist parties and movements its leaders felt were insufficiently radical.

The Peruvian government in the 1980s struggled to contain the Shining Path—the country's deeply ingrained inequalities and tensions along cultural and geographical lines made it fertile ground for a hard-left military movement. This has come to be called the nation's "Lost Decade." By 1990, the Shining Path either controlled or was active in nearly half of Peru — including parts of the Sechura Desert in the north where Fr. Prevost served.

The momentum shifted in the 1990s, however, when the Japanese-Peruvian prime minister Alberto Fujimori came to power. Fujimori combined a commitment to free-market capitalism with a brutal suppression of the Shining Path insurgency, becoming a popular but highly controversial figure in Peruvian life. Two years into his term, he plotted with the armed forces to dissolve the legislature, giving himself dictatorial authority.

The Fujimori government met the Shining Path's savage violence with extremism of its own, including torture and extrajudicial executions performed by government secret police — or death squads. Government and insurgent forces killed, maimed, and tortured with impunity. Among the civilians caught in the crossfire, the country's indigenous population suffered the most.

Over the decade Fujimori remained in power, these tactics, though deeply immoral, proved effective. By the time Fujimori was forced to leave office in 2000 — he fled the country under threat of prosecution for corruption and war crimes — the Shining Path had been reduced to irrelevancy, though it was still involved in some drug production in Peru's wild interior. Fujimori was eventually extradited to Peru, convicted of corruption and crimes against humanity, and imprisoned. The violence in the previous years had left more than seventy thousand dead.

It was into this political and social environment, a country in despair where violence lurked almost everywhere, that Leo arrived in Chulucanas in 1985, and then to Trujillo in 1988. Here, he would live and serve for the next decade.

Always an Augustinian

> You didn't know sometimes who you were talking to.... People didn't trust each other. They didn't know who were informants for the government or informants for the Sendero Luminoso. So people were afraid to talk; people were afraid to express themselves.[24]

That's how Bishop Turley described the uncertainty of life during Peru's civil war to *America* magazine. But the Church had an obligation not just to survive, but to continue to serve the spiritual and material needs of the people who were caught in the middle. And that's what Fr. Prevost—who always went by the Spanish version of his name, *Roberto*—did in Trujillo.

Trujillo is Peru's third most populous city, still in the country's north, but about two hundred miles south of Chulucanas. It's a fast-growing coastal city: it had under five hundred thousand residents when Fr. Prevost arrived in 1988 and has nearly a million residents today. The median income is about twelve thousand dollars per year—about a quarter of what it is in the capital of Lima—but much of the city consists of desperately poor slums. Nearly 80 percent of the population is Catholic.

It's hard to name a role Fr. Prevost did not fill while serving in Trujillo. He was the prior of the Augustinian community in the city, and a formation director for aspiring friars. He was an academic and spiritual instructor for his fellow friars. He was a judge in the archdiocesan ecclesiastical courts. But it's clear that his most important responsibilities, which illuminate key aspects of his character, were academic and pastoral.

Fr. Prevost was clearly an intellectual leader in Trujillo. He led the archdiocesan seminary and placed a particular emphasis on recruiting local men to the priesthood, to raise up a generation of Peruvian priests to serve their country. He also brought his Roman training from the Angelicum to Trujillo, teaching canon law, patristics, and moral theology.

When it came to the Peruvian political situation, Fr. Robert Prevost charted a middle path. Whereas some Catholics, including bishops, openly supported the Fujimori regime's crackdowns on Shining Path, he criticized the excesses of both sides. Although he clearly had no sympathy for the insane ideology and wanton violence of Shining Path, neither could he turn a blind eye to state-sponsored violence. And especially in the poor communities where he worked, serving everyone meant understanding political sympathies in all directions, even those he didn't share.

When, in 2017, a pardon was granted to Fujimori by then-president of Peru Pedro Pablo Kuczynski, then-Bishop Prevost of Chiclayo spoke out against the pardon but also the apparent lack of remorse on the part of Fujimori. "Perhaps," Bishop Prevost, said, "it would be more effective on his part to personally ask for forgiveness for some of the great injustices that were committed and for which he was tried." The pardon was eventually overturned and Fujimori returned to prison. He was released in 2023 and died the following year.

Fr. Robert Prevost served his flock at two parishes (fittingly) on the south side of Trujillo, about one mile apart: Nuestra Señora de Montserrat (Our Lady of Montserrat) and Santa Rita de Cascia — the same patron of the Augustinian church and school where he had worked in Chicago. Our Lady of Monserrat is painted bright pink on the outside and features tremendous rounded wood doors emblazoned with a cross. Santa Rita is a gated compound that has a mural of St. Augustine on the outer wall.

These weren't parishes that Fr. Prevost parachuted into: these were parishes he *built*. He also founded schools for his parishes. Every account of his pastoral service that has come out of Trujillo, and elsewhere in Peru, is exemplary — especially his service to the poor, and during emergencies, such as the periodic floods that strike the region.

One particular account, given to a Spanish language television station after Leo was elected, stands out. Hector Camacho served Fr. Prevost — or, rather, *Padre Roberto*, as he was known — as a member of the Cristo Rey Altar Boys club in Chulucanas. When Leo's mother, Mildred, died in 1990, Hector and his wife decided to name their unborn daughter in her honor, and asked Padre Roberto to serve as godfather, which he accepted.

That little girl, now a grown woman, was asked what it's like to be the pope's goddaughter. She replied:

> I've always, always said that I have my godfather's blessing.... I already admired him from childhood. He's been someone who has stayed present—with letters, with messages—and when he came to visit Chulucanas he would take time before each Mass to greet us. And the fact that he is now Pope—well, it feels nice to know that I've had that blessing from him since I was little.

Hector recalls Leo as a man who brought a feeling of peace and tranquility wherever he went, including especially the poor villages around Chulucanas (and, later, Trujillo and Chiclayo). When the priest would approach, sometimes on horse or mule, members of the village young and old would shout, "Padre Roberto!" and run to embrace him. He was seen, it is not too much to say, as a living saint.

In recent years, both churches Padre Roberto served in Trujillo have featured advertisements for the local St. Augustine College, featuring the tagline, *Una vez Agustino ... siempre Agustinos!* That is: "Once an Augustinian, always an Augustinian!" In Trujillo, as across northern Peru, the legacy of the Augustinians—and of "Padre Roberto"—is everywhere.

In the years to come, he would extend that service even further, as Bishop Roberto.

CHAPTER 5

Christ in Peru

Peru has given the Church two of the most remarkable saints in the Western Hemisphere, and in all Church history: St. Martin de Porres and St. Rose of Lima. Now, this beautiful land has given the Church a pope.

The Church came to Peru in the early sixteenth century alongside Spanish conquistadors. It was here that Francisco Pizarro encountered the Inca, one of the most extraordinary civilizations in human history. The Inca spanned from present-day Colombia all the way down the South American Pacific coast to roughly Santiago, Chile: a 2,500-mile empire. But their heartland was Peru, and in particular Cuzco, in the southern highlands.

Very quickly, imperial Spanish society took root there, eventually headquartered at Lima, on the arid coastline. And then, remarkably, within just a few generations this colonial city became the home of two extraordinary contemporary saints, both members of the Third Order of St. Dominic: Martin de Porres and Rose of Lima.

Both Martin de Porres and Rose of Lima exemplify an intense spirituality that seems to have arisen providentially in their particular place and time and has imprinted itself on the DNA of Peruvian Catholicism from the very beginning. In Peru, there are no half measures: you're either all out, or you're all in.

Saint of the North

Fr. Prevost left Peru for the second time in 1998 when he was elected prior provincial of the Order of St. Augustine's Province of Our Mother of Good Counsel based in Chicago. Three years later, he was elected prior general of the Order of St. Augustine and served two consecutive six-year terms until 2013. He then served from 2013 to 2014 as director of formation at the Convent of St. Augustine in Chicago, and as first councilor and provincial vicar of the Province of Our Mother of Good Counsel.

Fr. Prevost had assumed his time in Peru was done, but after fifteen years of service to the Augustinian Order outside the country, Pope Francis sent him back.

The future pope returned to Peru in 2014, where he became apostolic administrator of the Chiclayo diocese after the age-forced resignation of Bishop Jesús Moliné Labarte. On December 12 of that year—the feast of Our Lady of Guadalupe, Patroness of the Americas—he was consecrated a bishop in the immense Cathedral of St. Mary in Chiclayo. This colonial-neoclassical masterpiece was started in 1869 but only finished in 1939 and was based on designs of Gustave Eiffel, most famous for a certain tower in France. Then on September 26, 2015, Pope Francis officially named him bishop of Chiclayo, the fifth most populated city in Peru with over six hundred thousand inhabitants. From 2020 to

2021, he was also the apostolic administrator of the Peruvian diocese of Callao.

Years later, Prevost said that he never expected to be made a bishop after Pope Francis was elected in 2013. He described some difficult interactions he had with Francis when he was Archbishop Bergoglio of Buenos Aires, Argentina. In a conversation at a parish in Illinois in 2024, then-Cardinal Prevost revealed that the two had butted heads over an assignment for an Augustinian friar in Bergoglio's diocese — and that Prevost, then prior general of the Order, had prevailed. Later, though, it seems that Prevost intervened on Bergoglio's behalf in some other Church matter, and so the new pope thought well of him.

As a bishop, he was willing to speak out in defense of Church teaching in key areas, including gender ideology and the defense of the unborn. While bishop of Chiclayo, he publicly opposed a government initiative to promote gender ideology teachings in schools. "The promotion of gender ideology," he said, "is confusing, because it seeks to create genders that don't exist."[25]

Similarly, he was an ardent supporter of the pro-life cause in Peru. In a homily in Chiclayo in 2019, he preached against what Pope Francis termed a throwaway culture, saying, "We cannot build a just society if we discard the weakest — whether the child in the womb or the elderly in their frailty — for they are both gifts from God."

As with every position Leo has held, he was quickly elevated to further leadership roles. In 2018, that meant serving as a vice president of the Peruvian Episcopal Conference, which includes leaders of more than forty dioceses. He also served as a member of the economic council and as president of the Commission for Culture and Education.

But these titles were never what Bishop Prevost was known for in Peru: that, rather, was his constant presence among his flock. Although the bishop was entitled to a chauffeur, he chose to drive around Chiclayo and its countryside himself. And if the car broke down, he was also the first to dig in to fix it—and the first you'd trust with trying.

When he visited those communities no car could reach, he ably mounted a horse or mule to complete the task. He traversed the Peruvian highlands on horseback—and didn't look or feel one bit out of place. "Even the bishops of Peru called him the saint, the Saint of the North, and he had time for everyone," the Augustinian Fr. Alexander Lam told the Associated Press in Rome. "He was the person who would find you along the way. He was this kind of bishop."[26]

Nothing demonstrated Bishop Prevost's desire to be close to his people, and his commitment to delivering material aid, than his service during the periodic floods that rush through the valleys and scour the flatlands. These images, too, of the determined bishop with pants tucked into tall plastic boots wading through floodwaters, have become indelible. In 2017, it was El Niño. In 2022, it was a tropical cyclone. But no matter the cause of the emergency, he was present.

And then there was the COVID pandemic. Peru's restrictions on daily life were particularly draconian, leaving the faithful without access to the sacraments for nine months. Yet people close to Leo during that time remember a man unafraid of the illness and of the people. "Bishop Prevost was never the kind of bishop who gave orders from behind a desk. He was the face of Christ, the one who went out into the mud to help his people," Janinna Sesa Córdova, who led Cáritas Chiclayo at the time, told Ines San Martin of OSV News.[27]

In the north of Peru, when COVID was at its worst, families whose loved ones depended on oxygen were running out. So Bishop Prevost created and led the Oxygen of Hope campaign, which led, Sesa recalled, to being "able to purchase two medicinal oxygen plants and provide free care to hundreds of families."

In the same story by San Martin, there's an interesting detail that reminds us that Leo — although renowned for his commitment to material aid — was still, first, a priest of Jesus Christ. Aldo Llanos, a professor of philosophy and anthropology at the University of Piura, said of Leo that he would happily come out to serve the people "in boots and a poncho." But "when it was time for Mass, he was impeccably vested."[28]

Questionable Abuse Cases

There have been rumblings that Prevost was too passive in investigating claims of clergy sexual abuse while serving as bishop of Chiclayo. The claims stem from accusations of abuse made against the diocese in 2022 by three sisters regarding alleged crimes of abuse by a priest in 2004 when the girls were minors. The sisters alleged that the Church investigation undertaken on Prevost's watch was insufficient and that the accused continued to celebrate Mass.

Similar accusations were made regarding his time as prior provincial of the Order of St. Augustine's Province of Our Mother of Good Counsel in Chicago. In 2000, he allegedly permitted an Augustinian priest accused of the sexual abuse of minors to reside at St. John Stone Friary in Chicago under supervision. The accused priest had been suspended from public ministry since 1991 due to credible accusations that he had sexually abused minors, and Prevost was later criticized because of the friary's location close to a school, although this was not a violation of canon law.

Regarding the later accusations in Chiclayo, Prevost's successor as bishop in that diocese, Edinson Farfán, defended his predecessor at a press conference about the issue, declaring, "That's a lie. He [Pope Leo XIV] has listened, he has respected the processes, and this process is still ongoing ... believe me, I am the most interested person in justice being served and, above all, in being able to help the victims."[29]

For its part, the Press Office of the Holy See issued a statement pointing to a 2023 declaration by the Office of Social Communications of the Diocese of Chiclayo that, "After receiving the complaints, the accused priest was summoned and asked to leave the parish and cease exercising his ministry. A preliminary investigation was initiated and then sent to the Holy See."[30] The 2023 statement also noted that the "Dicastery for the Doctrine of the Faith, seeing that the accusations brought against the accused priest have not been sufficiently proven, consequently decided to close the case pro nunc."

In 2023, after being appointed to the post of prefect for the Dicastery for Bishops, then-Archbishop Prevost was interviewed by Vatican News. He was asked about the Church's response to the abuse crisis, the responsibility of bishops, and the need to change the mentality when it comes to confronting abuse. He said in part:

> There are places where good work has already been done for years and the rules are being put into practice. At the same time, I believe that there is still much to learn.
>
> I am talking about the urgency and responsibility of accompanying victims. One of the difficulties that many times arise is that the bishop must be close to his priests, as I have already said, and he must be close to the victims. Some recommend that it not be the bishop directly who receives the victims; but we cannot close our hearts, the door of the Church, to people who have suffered from abuse....
>
> Certainly, there are many differences between one culture and another on how one reacts in these situations. In some countries, the taboo of talking about the subject has already been broken somewhat, while there are other places where victims, or victims' families, would never want to talk about the abuse they have suffered.
>
> In any case, silence is not an answer. Silence is not the solution. We must be transparent and honest, we must accompany and assist the victims, because otherwise their wounds will never heal. There is a great responsibility in this, for all of us.[31]

Always Jesus

In contrast to the allegations, Pope Leo XIV's spiritual service to the people of Chiclayo hasn't gotten as much attention from the largely secular press—but it's clear it wasn't just central, but foundational to his ministry. Although he apparently met graciously with Fr. Gustavo Gutiérrez, the primary founder of liberation theology, there is no evidence whatsoever that Bishop Prevost considered his temporal ministry—that is to say, his material support for the people—to be more important than, or even on par with, his spiritual ministry.

Rather, the material service was always inspired by, built on the firm foundation of, and pointed his flock toward the Divine Person of Jesus Christ. Take the pandemic. Although Bishop Prevost organized lifesaving medical supplies, he also took to the streets—with the Blessed Sacrament. In an echo of Pope Francis's own extraordinary Urbi et Orbi blessing in March 2020, Leo blessed Chiclayo with Jesus held in a beautiful monstrance. In so doing he also brought consolation to his flock, who went nine months without communal gatherings.

Leo is also said to support a historic eucharistic miracle that occurred in Eten, a town just south of Chiclayo, in 1649. According to the Real Presence Eucharistic Education and Adoration Association:

> The first apparition of the Divine Child in the Most Holy Sacrament took place on the night of June 2, 1649, during the Vespers and the solemn exposition in honor of the feast of Corpus Christi.

> At the end of the service, the Franciscan monk Jerome de Silva Manrique, was about to return the monstrance to the tabernacle, but he suddenly stopped. In the Host there appeared the brilliant face of a Child, framed by thick brown curls falling to the shoulders. All the faithful present in the church observed the same vision.[32]

A similar event occurred a few weeks later:

> According to the testimony of Brother Marco Lopez, superior of the convent in Chiclayo, during the exposition of the Most Holy Sacrament, "The Divine Child Jesus again appeared in the Host, dressed in a purple tunic. Beneath it he wore a shirt up to the middle of the chest, according to the custom of the South American Indians." Through this sign, the Divine Child wanted to identify with the Mochican inhabitants of Eten, to demonstrate His love for them. In the same apparition, which lasted about 15 minutes, many also saw appearing in the Host three small white hearts, united among themselves. These symbolized the Three Persons of the Holy Trinity: the Father, the Son, and the Holy Spirit, present in the consecrated Host. To this day, the feast in honor of the miracle of the Divine Child of Eten, continues to attract thousands of faithful yearly.[33]

The people of Eten have long hoped their miracle would receive official recognition from the Church, and that their town would be recognized as a eucharistic city. Leo's elevation to the Throne of Peter may make that more likely.

As bishop, Leo was also said to be gentle but uncompromising on matters of Catholic truth. "He also said things firmly when he saw something that was not right or something that was not in accordance with the things of the Church," Fr. Elmer Uchofen told the New York Times.[34] Others report that Bishop Prevost did not hesitate to privately correct people, including sending "several harsh letters," San Martin reports, to those who participated in corruption and other illegal and immoral activity. In this, he is reminiscent of St. Ambrose, bishop of Milan, who rebuked the Emperor Theodosius for his immoral actions, resulting in the emperor's meek penance and return to the Church.

Leo also had particular affection for the nuns under his care in Chiclayo, especially (of course) the Augustinians. Multiple communities remember him fondly as a faithful brother who encouraged them in their individual and communal charisms and callings.

"He has shared meals with us, celebrated with us, accompanied us, encouraged us, and that is moving for us, because he has done so in his simplicity, with trust, with prayer," Sr. Marlene Quispe told Rhina Guidos of the Global Sisters Report. "He was a man who listened a lot, who helped others discern, whose words were fundamental in creating communion. And he was a true brother."[35]

Here is how Leo responded when asked by an Augustinian publication, shortly after being made a cardinal in 2023, what it means to be a good bishop:

> To be a good shepherd means to be able to walk side-by-side with the People of God and to live close to them, not to be isolated.... A bishop, therefore, has to have many skills. He has to know how to govern, to administer, to organise and to know how to deal with people. But if I had to point out one trait above all others, it is that he must proclaim Jesus Christ and live the faith so that the faithful see in his witness an incentive to them to want to be an ever more active part of the Church that Jesus Christ himself founded. In just a few words: to help people come to know Christ through the gift of faith.[36]

There is no better proof that Bishop Prevost lived out his own definition of the good bishop than the reaction of his flock to his elevation to the Chair of Peter. Hundreds of thousands of Peruvians gathered in the streets of Chiclayo to celebrate, without hesitation. And then there were the seminarians, who were videotaped watching Cardinal Dominique Mamberti, the protodeacon, intone, *Habemus papam*. When he read the name *Robertum Franciscum*, a tremor went through the room. And when he said *Prevost*, it exploded as if Peru had just won the World Cup.

He never forgot his beloved Peru or his diocese. On the day of his election, when he delivered his first *Urbi et Orbi* address, Pope Leo XIV included a special greeting to his old diocese in Spanish:

> *Y si me permiten también una palabra, un saludo a todos y en modo particular a mi querida diócesis de*

Chiclayo, en el Perú, donde un pueblo fiel ha acompañado a su obispo, ha compartido su fe y ha dado tanto, tanto, para seguir siendo Iglesia fiel de Jesucristo.

And if you also allow me a brief word, a greeting to everyone and in particular to my beloved Diocese of Chiclayo, in Peru, where a faithful people has accompanied its Bishop, shared its faith and given so much, so much, to continue being a faithful Church of Jesus Christ.

CHAPTER 6

A Missionary's Heart

When Pope Leo XIV stepped onto the loggia of St. Peter's Basilica for the first time, there was one word anyone who knew him expected to hear: *missionary*. In fact, they got it twice.

> I also thank my brother Cardinals, who have chosen me to be the Successor of Peter and to walk together with you as a Church, united, ever pursuing peace and justice, ever seeking to act as men and women faithful to Jesus Christ, in order to proclaim the Gospel without fear, to be *missionaries*.
>
> I am an Augustinian, a son of Saint Augustine, who once said, "With you I am a Christian, and for you I am a bishop." In this sense, all of us can journey together toward the homeland that God has prepared for us.
>
> A special greeting to the Church of Rome! Together, we must look for ways to be a *missionary* Church, a Church that builds bridges and encourages dialogue, a Church ever open to welcoming, like this Square with its open arms, all those who are in need of our charity, our presence, our readiness to dialogue and our love. [Emphasis added]

Of all the roles Leo has played, from teacher to pastor to bishop to pope, it is that of the missionary that is closest to his heart and that he brings to everything else he does. "But of course," Leo said to a parish in Illinois just last year, "the part of my ministry that most shaped my life was Peru."[37]

Leo is the first pope to have served as a missionary since the early Church. Through this remarkable fact, the Lord is communicating clearly to the Church that the *entire* Church is now called in a special way to be missionaries to a post-Christian world. Our mission field isn't just rural Peru or the desiccated South Side of Chicago: it's the entire world—and in a particular way the remnants of Christendom.

Worldwide Mission Field

Peru is a land of sharp contrasts, between the lowlands and highlands, the desert and the rainforest, the rich and the poor. Bishop Prevost navigated these contrasts expertly and became a unifying force across them—with that unity rooted in Christ, just as St. Augustine would have it. Although the material needs of the people might be different in different places and at different times, and their spiritual needs might also need to be fulfilled in different manners, what they all needed most of all—what they needed from their pastor—was Jesus.

This raises another contrast: that between Peru and Leo's home country of the United States. Although America has its share of poverty, even destitution, it cannot compare with northern Peru, where so many people—perhaps even a majority—live precariously. They know that one flood, one lost job or economic recession, one poor harvest, one accident can mean the loss of everything. Everything material, that is.

It's not hard, then, to draw another contrast, one that reflects more poorly on the United States. In Peru, Leo was surrounded by troubles, to be sure, but also great faith, anchored in a supernatural relationship with God that transcended those troubles. In America, Leo saw, and sees, great wealth, but also terrible spiritual impoverishment. In other words, he sees a civilization in need of a missionary Church.

"Our church is missionary by its very essence." Bishop Dan Turley told *America* magazine. "We were born out of the mission: 'Go forth, teach and baptize in the name of the Father, the Son and the Holy Spirit.' ... If we ever lose that, we would not be the church of Christ."[38] Thinking in these terms, then, the loss of Christendom and the loss of faith in the rich West are, although tragic, also an opportunity and an invitation—to remember and to recover what the Church is meant to be.

Some have speculated that the missionary pope will emphasize expanding mission work in the so-called Global South—those developing nations in Africa, Asia, and elsewhere where the Church is growing by leaps and bounds. That may be so. But Leo's understanding of a missionary Church is not going to be sequestered to the usual places.

He has seen the collapse of the Church in his hometown firsthand. He knows that Chicago is at least as much of a mission field as Chiclayo. And in his Augustinian spirituality, tested and strengthened in *Peru profundo*, he has the answer: unity in Christ.

Embracing Mystery

Many times—not every time, but many times—after a pope is elected, all the previous speculation about the politics of the conclave look a little ridiculous. Because, once it's over, it feels like the answer was obvious all along. This is shaping up to be one of those cases.

Cardinal Robert Prevost entered the conclave with the most diverse experience of the Church around the world of any member of the College. From the American Midwest to the Peruvian north to Rome and beyond, he has walked with the people of God in a tremendous, and truly unique, variety of ways. "Recognising the great richness of diversity within the People of God is tremendously useful because it makes us more sensitive when it comes time to better reach out and respond to what they expect from us," Leo has said of his own experiences.

> There are many different cultures, many different languages, many different circumstances around the world where the Church responds. So when we list our priorities and weigh up the challenges before us we have to be aware that the urgencies of Italy, Spain, the United States, Peru or China, for example, are almost certainly not the same *except in one thing*: the underlying challenge that Christ left to us to preach the Gospel and that this is the same everywhere. [emphasis added][39]

That is the same everywhere. Here is the fundamental insight Leo brings to the Church in the twenty-first century, remarkably simple yet utterly necessary and impossibly profound: everywhere, in every circumstance, in every culture, in every home and every village, in the cities and in the fields, the world needs Christ.

And nothing can replace Him. In Peru, Leo would have had to deal with politics and ideologies of power vying to replace Christ, with traditional and syncretic religions that denied or deemphasized Him, and later smartphones and mass media, which have colonized nearly every niche of human civilization. In America, Leo sees politics as well, but in different ways, and also the impact of mass media to a much greater degree. But he also sees wealth and distraction and nihilism — the kind of ideology of nothingness that can only arise in a civilization that has so much.

The circumstances are different, but the solution is the same — though its application must be tailored to particular circumstances. The proposal of Christ in Peru will look different from the proposal of Christ in America. The former, for instance, will be much more likely accompanied by material support. The latter — we can surmise from some of Leo's early papal remarks — should be accompanied by beauty and mystery, antidotes to a culture of backhanded irony and scientific certainty.

Here, for instance, is an excerpt from Leo's remarks to a representative of the Eastern Catholic Churches, only six days into his papacy:

> The contribution that the Christian East can offer us today is immense! We have great need to

> recover the sense of mystery that remains alive in your liturgies, liturgies that engage the human person in his or her entirety, that sing of the beauty of salvation and evoke a sense of wonder at how God's majesty embraces our human frailty! It is likewise important to rediscover, especially in the Christian West, a sense of the primacy of God, the importance of mystagogy and the values so typical of Eastern spirituality: constant intercession, penance, fasting, and weeping for one's own sins and for those of all humanity (*penthos*)! It is vital, then, that you preserve your traditions without attenuating them, for the sake perhaps of practicality or convenience, lest they be corrupted by the mentality of consumerism and utilitarianism.[40]

That last line is particularly pointed, begging for tradition and mystery to remain uncorrupted by consumerism and utilitarianism. For Leo, this is how we propose Christ anew to the world, but in particular in those places that have rejected Him. Or, rather, rejected a safe, sanitized, diluted version of the good news—the charismatic holy man rather than the Son of God.

That claim, that Jesus Christ is the Son of God, was scandalous when it was first made, and then over the centuries it became taken for granted. That was good, a product of the success of the Church. That was Christendom. But now it is scandalous once again, and so it *should* appear strange and mysterious by contemporary standards, just as the first

Christian missionaries were strange and mysterious in Peru half a millennium ago.

Missionary Church

In illo Uno unum. "In the One, we are one." But what does the word *in* mean? First, it means being in communion with Christ, which means being in communion with His Church. Second, and more fundamentally, it means loving the one God, which is how we accept His invitation to enter into His life through grace.

And essential to loving God is loving His truth — that is to say, the doctrines of the Church. It is clear that Leo does not believe that diluting the Church's immutable teachings — making them palatable for contemporary tastes — is the path to unity. In fact, this approach makes unity less likely, because it leaves the People of God disagreeing about who Christ is and what He stands for. That is the facade of unity but not the genuine article. And there is no evidence Leo has ever sought this false compromise.

Therefore it is the task of the missionary — that is, it is the task of all of us — to spread the love of God and the truth of God, and in so doing to expand the communion of Christ and His Church. This is the perpetual missionary calling of the Church, but it is also the special purpose to which we are called by a missionary pope.

Here we do see continuity between Pope Francis and Pope Leo XIV, even though there appear to be significant differences in approach — most notably Leo's embrace of traditional papal vestments, blessings, and so on. Just last year, then-Cardinal

Prevost said it was precisely his missionary background that brought him to Francis's attention to run the Vatican's bishops office: "He called me ... specifically because he didn't want someone from the Roman Curia to take on this role. He wanted a missionary. He wanted someone from outside."[41]

According to an Augustinian sister in Chiclayo, however, Prevost wasn't sold on the idea of going back to Rome. He loved Peru, being a missionary bishop in a beautiful land of contrasts, being close to his flock. Sr. Marlene Quispe reported to the *Global Sisters Report* that this is how he expressed himself: "I feel like a missionary and I don't see myself in Rome, but I have prayed and perhaps now what I have to be is a missionary in Rome. *There is also a mission to be accomplished there*" (emphasis added).[42]

There may not be a more important single sentence for understanding Leo XIV's vision for the Church, and for each member of the Body of Christ. Yes, he loved being a missionary in mission territory. But everywhere is mission territory!

In fact, even Rome is mission territory.

PART 3

ROME: THE ETERNAL CITY

CHAPTER 7

An Experienced Churchman

Pope Leo XIV has broken ground in multiple ways: He's the first American pope ever, and the first missionary pope since the early Church. But he is also, like so many popes before him, a man of the institutional Catholic Church.

Just beyond the south colonnade that encloses St. Peter's Square, and that defines the border of Vatican City, there's a short street, just a few hundred feet long, that connects the nerve center of the Catholic Church to a major Roman thoroughfare. This little road is called the Piazza del Sant'Uffizio, or Holy Office Square, and for nearly all the many years he's spent in Rome, it was Leo's address.

On the east side of the Sant'Uffizio is the international headquarters of the Order of St. Augustine, which includes residences, offices, a monastery, the Pontifical Patristic Institute, the Augustinianum (a school of theology focusing on patristics, or the study of the Church Fathers), and the Chapel of St. Monica. Here, Leo celebrated Mass while visiting his confreres just five days into his papacy. He knew the building well, because he would have lived there during his studies at the Angelicum, and it was his home and office during his twelve years as prior general of the Order.

On the west side of Sant'Uffizio is the building for which the street is named: the Palazzo del Sant'Uffizio, the Palace of the Holy Office. This is the headquarters of the Dicastery for the Doctrine of the Faith, the office charged with safeguarding and also articulating and clarifying the teachings of the Church. The dicastery or curial office, known in history under various names, including the Holy Office and the Congregation for the Doctrine of the Faith, is housed in a large palazzo resting right at the entrance into the Vatican, just to the south of St. Peter's Basilica and very close to the famed Paul VI Hall, where the pope will hold some of his general audiences. Today, the building serves several purposes, including as a residence for some Vatican officials. Among them was prefect for the Dicastery for Bishops, Cardinal Robert Francis Prevost.

It seems fitting for a man so consistently described as grounded that he would have such a stable home in Rome. Further, his straddling of the Piazza del Sant'Uffizio evokes his own straddling of worlds: America and Peru, pastor and missionary and executive, the Church and the world. It was fitting, too, that he should live literally in the shadow of the basilica and in sight of St. Peter's Square, both of which he would one day call his own.

Here once again we see the theme of unity and charity: Leo's work in the world, both spiritual and material, was only valuable if it was anchored in love of God. And although he would have preferred to keep performing that work in his adopted home of Peru, God and His Church called Leo to bring that missionary spirit to the universal Church in the Eternal City.

Called to Rome

Leo's experience in Rome began all the way back in 1982, when his Augustinian superiors recognized his talent and sent him to the prestigious Pontifical University of St. Thomas Aquinas, the Angelicum, to continue his studies. He completed his licentiate in canon law in 1984, giving him the privilege to serve in various capacities in ecclesiastical courts. But he wasn't done: after making his first mission trip to Peru in 1985 and 1986, Leo, then Fr. Prevost, completed his doctorate at the Angelicum in 1987.

Both studying at the Angelicum and his course of study indicate not just a sharp mind, but a precise, orderly mind. This is something that Leo's teachers and friends noticed about him throughout his life: his missionary's heart is complemented by a professor's intellect. Not just a professor's — a practitioner's, as well. Unsurprisingly, Leo's doctoral dissertation regarded Augustinian matters: "The Office and Authority of the Local Prior in the Order of St. Augustine."

He would go on to put his canon law training to use extensively, including as a teacher at the seminary in Trujillo. His legal expertise was also essential in devising protocols for responding to claims of sexual abuse for the Peruvian bishops, as well as in his time as prior general of the Augustinians.

Leo took his first major leadership role with his order in 1998, when he was named prior provincial for the Midwest Augustinians of Our Mother of Good Counsel. This brought him home from Trujillo to suburban Chicago—though the job also included responsibility for the province's missions, which kept him on the move. Then, in 2001, he was elected prior general for the international Augustinian Order, a role he would hold for two consecutive six-year terms.

As prior general, Leo was responsible for nearly three thousand Augustinians, including friars and nuns, active in dozens of settings—schools, colleges, monasteries, parishes, missions—in forty-seven countries around the world. This introduced him to numerous cultures and contexts around the world. In addition to Peru, the Catholic News Agency reports that Leo has visited Australia, the Democratic Republic of the Congo, India, Indonesia, Kenya, Nigeria, the Philippines, South Korea, and Tanzania.

In addition to English and Spanish, he is fluent in Italian, French, and Portuguese. He is also capable in Quechua, an indigenous language in Peru, as well as Latin, as the world witnessed when he chanted the *Regina Coeli* from the loggia of St. Peter's on the first Sunday of his pontificate.

Running an international religious order comes with extraordinary responsibilities. The Augustinians' vow of obedience gives the prior general the power to direct the lives of thousands of friars, while navigating the financial and bureaucratic complexities that come with any large international organization. Yet, remarkably, Fr. Donald Reilly—the former prior provincial for the eastern U.S. Province of St. Thomas of Villanova — reports that Fr. Prevost earned the respect of every person he dealt with. Somehow, in twelve years of hard decisions, no one in the Order felt he had done them an injustice.

The prior general in those years had the particularly sensitive task of merging provinces and closing ministries, due to long-term reductions in the number of religious. Fr. Reilly describes — in a way echoed by so many others who worked with Leo — a form of deliberation that was extremely effective in achieving, if not consensus, then at least peace with his own final decision.

Leo would first listen to what every person had to say and learn from it. Then he would synthesize what he had heard and learned and demonstrate to everyone in his own speech that he understood their positions and concerns. Everyone wouldn't just *feel* heard; they'd *know* they were heard. Then, when Leo made his final decision — and he is decisive — it was truly informed by all available information and perspectives, and participants were ready to move forward.

At a press conference held at the Pontifical North American College in Rome after the conclave, the American cardinals who had just taken part in the conclave gave their thoughts on the new pope. Cardinal Joseph W. Tobin of Newark, New Jersey, said he has known the new pontiff for thirty years, including the time they were in Rome together in the late 1990s and early 2000s, when Tobin was superior general of the Redemptorists and Fr. Prevost was superior of the Augustinians.

Cardinal Tobin has also served as a member of the Dicastery for Bishops, and worked with then-Cardinal Robert F. Prevost when he was prefect.

Cardinal Tobin described the new pope's leadership style, saying, "I don't think he's one that likes to pick fights, but he is not one to back down if the cause is just. And I guess the last thing I'd say about Bob is that he really is a listener, and then he acts."[43]

It's not hard to see in this a model of so-called "synodality" that simultaneously listens to concerns in a democratic way but decides in a hierarchical way. That is, a mode of synodality that respects everybody, including the distinct role of spiritual leaders in the Church.

Fr. Prevost's time as prior general also coincided with the deluge of revelations of sexual abuse in the Church, which began in 2002. He is said to have been proactive: although religious orders did not immediately come under scrutiny the way dioceses did, he did not wait for the spotlight to shine on his Order. Fr. Reilly reports that Leo worked with secular professionals to create safety and reporting protocols that also respected the distinctly communal nature of Augustinian life and spirituality.

A Memorable Intervention

It was during Fr. Prevost's second term as Augustinian prior general that Pope Benedict XVI called the Synod on the New Evangelization, to explore how the Church can propose Christ anew to those who had fallen away from the Church. During one of the synod sessions, Fr. Prevost delivered a striking reflection on the way mass media competes with and ultimately replaces the Christian message with secularism, consumerism, and immorality. Here is that intervention in its entirety:

> Western mass media is extraordinarily effective in fostering within the general public enormous sympathy for beliefs and practices that are at odds with the Gospel—for example, abortion, homosexual lifestyle, euthanasia. Religion is at best tolerated by mass media as tame and quaint when it does not actively oppose positions on ethical issues that the media have embraced as their own. However, when religious voices are raised in opposition to these positions, mass media can target religion, labeling it as ideological and insensitive in regard to the so-called vital needs of people in the contemporary world.
>
> The sympathy for anti-Christian lifestyle choices that mass media fosters is so brilliantly and artfully ingrained in the viewing public that when people hear the Christian message, it often inevitably seems ideological and emotionally cruel by contrast to the ostensible humaneness of the anti-Christian perspective. Catholic pastors who preach against the legalization of abortion or the redefinition of marriage are portrayed as being ideologically driven, severe, and uncaring—not because of anything they say or do, but because their audiences contrast their message with the sympathetic, caring tones of

media–produced images of human beings who, because they are caught in morally complex life situations, opt for choices that are made to appear as healthful and good.

Note, for example, how alternative families comprised of same-sex partners and their adopted children are so benignly and sympathetically portrayed in television programs and cinema today. If the new evangelization is going to counter these mass media-produced distortions of religious and ethical reality successfully, pastors, preachers, teachers and catechists are going to have to become far more informed about the context of evangelizing in a world dominated by mass media.

The church fathers offered a formidable response to those non-Christian and anti-Christian literary and rhetorical forces at work throughout the Roman Empire in shaping the religious and ethical imaginations of the day. The *Confessions* of St. Augustine, with its central image of the *cor inquietum* [restless heart], has shaped the way that Western Christians and non-Christians reimagine the adventure of religious conversion. In his *City of God*, Augustine used the tale of Alexander the Great's encounter with a captured pirate to ironize the supposed moral legitimacy of the Roman Empire.

Church fathers, among them John Chrysostom, Ambrose, Leo the Great, Gregory of Nyssa, were not great rhetoricians insofar as they were great preachers. They were great preachers because they were first great rhetoricians. In other words, their evangelizing was successful in great part because they understood the foundations of social communication appropriate to the world in which they lived. Consequently, they understood with enormous precision the techniques through which popular religious and ethical imaginations of their day were manipulated by the centers of secular power in that world.

Moreover, the Church should resist the temptation to believe that it can compete with modern mass media by turning the sacred liturgy into spectacle. Here again, church fathers such as Tertullian remind us today that visual spectacle is the domain of the *saeculum* [the secular realm], and that our proper mission is to introduce people to the nature of mystery as an antidote to spectacle. As a consequence, evangelization in the modern world must find the appropriate means for redirecting public attention away from spectacle and into mystery.

While much secular media attention has been paid to the first paragraph, where Fr. Prevost expresses disapproval of "homosexual lifestyle," this misses the most interesting aspects of his speech: his deep reflection on the interaction between modern mass media and the proclamation of the good news of Jesus Christ. He advises the Church to look to its roots, when great men like Ambrose and Augustine received training in rhetoric—the timeless study of communication and persuasion that was, also, cutting-edge at the time—so they could become better preachers.

In a particular way, the future pope admonishes the Church not to seek to compete with secular media on its own terms, but rather to offer an alternative in the way proper to the Christian message, and the Person of Christ Himself. That is, not "spectacle," but "mystery." Pope Leo returned to this theme, as we have seen, in one of the very first speeches of his pontificate, when he addressed leaders of Eastern Catholic churches about maintaining their spiritual and liturgical patrimony.

Fr. Prevost's remarks were entitled "The Counterculture of the New Evangelization," and clearly indicate—once again—a man not looking to compromise with modern secularism. Rather, he regards contemporary civilization, especially in the West, as mission territory.

This was stressed in his audience with the media a few days after his election. He thanked the press for their hard work in covering the interregnum and then talked about the challenges of communication in the modern world:

> Today, one of the most important challenges is to promote communication that can bring us out of the "Tower of Babel" in which we sometimes find ourselves, out of the confusion

of loveless languages that are often ideological or partisan. Therefore, your service, with the words you use and the style you adopt, is crucial. As you know, communication is not only the transmission of information, but it is also the creation of a culture, of human and digital environments that become spaces for dialogue and discussion. In looking at how technology is developing, this mission becomes ever more necessary. I am thinking in particular of artificial intelligence, with its immense potential, which nevertheless requires responsibility and discernment in order to ensure that it can be used for the good of all, so that it can benefit all of humanity. This responsibility concerns everyone in proportion to his or her age and role in society.[44]

Roman Mission

After completing his twelve years as prior general, Leo returned briefly to Chicago before being sent to Chiclayo by Pope Francis. Then, in 2023, he was called to Rome again — this time for good.

Francis had already shown interest in the future pope's potential for Roman responsibilities. In 2019, the pope appointed him as a member of the Congregation for the Clergy. The next year, he also joined the Congregation for Bishops. (*congregations* were renamed *dicasteries* in 2022.) This gave the

Peruvian bishop some experience in the Vatican bureaucracy of the Roman Curia.

He did not want to leave when Pope Francis asked him to become the prefect, or head, of the Dicastery for Bishops in April 2023. But, as we have seen, he felt—rightly—the Lord was providing him with new mission territory. The job also came with a promotion: Francis made Leo a cardinal, typical for prefects of Vatican offices, in September 2023.

Initially, as was typical for members of the Curia appointed to the College of Cardinals, Prevost was named a cardinal deacon and given the titular church in Rome of Santa Monica. In early 2025, however, he was transferred to the rank of Cardinal Bishop of Albano, making him one of the most senior cardinals despite having been a member of the College for less than two years. It was a statement of Pope Francis's esteem and confidence in the prefect.

As prefect, it was Leo's responsibility to oversee leadership of five thousand dioceses and other Church territories. That meant everything from training and (essentially) continuing education for existing bishops to the most visible part of the job: advising the Holy Father about whom to name to dioceses over much of the world. (Some bishops are the responsibility of other Vatican offices, such as the Dicastery for the Evangelization of Peoples, which oversees the Church's vast mission field.) That means that much of the job involves understanding the pope's priorities and helping him to fulfill those priorities.

In the politics of the Church, it can be difficult to attribute any particular decision to any particular person (except, of course, the pope himself). Sometimes even prefects of dicasteries are bypassed or overruled. While some observers have credited (or blamed) then-Cardinal Prevost for a variety of appointments under Francis, it's important to remember, as Prevost would constantly say when describing his work, that the pope, and only the pope, has the final word.

As prefect, however, Leo's responsibilities ranged far beyond America. It was here that he developed relationships and got his most intense education yet in the administration of the Church—applying and supplementing his American background and his Peruvian experience. It was all this together that attracted the attention of the cardinal electors who would choose the next pope.

CHAPTER 8

The Conclave

ON FEBRUARY 14, 2025, Pope Francis was taken to Gemelli Hospital and admitted for respiratory distress as a result of a cold. Over the next few days, his condition deteriorated with the start of pneumonia in both lungs. The Holy Father never recovered.

Brought back to the Casa Santa Marta in the Vatican on March 23, Pope Francis made several public appearances, but he had not fully recovered his voice and remained frail. His last appearance was on Easter Sunday when he took part in the traditional *Urbi et Orbi* blessing from the loggia of St. Peter's Basilica.

His condition declined again over the next several hours, and early on April 21, he suffered a stroke and respiratory collapse that claimed his life around 6:30 a.m.

With the passing of Pope Francis, the Church entered into the *sede vacante*, the interregnum when the Chair of St. Peter is empty and the Church's affairs are placed into the care of the College of Cardinals. Daily preparations for the funeral and subsequent conclave were guided by the Cardinal Camerlengo, the Irish-American Cardinal Kevin Farrell.

Over the previous years—given Pope Francis's slow but palpable medical decline—speculation had increased about possible successors. Talk about *papabile*—cardinals who might be suitable successors to the papacy—is a longstanding reality of the human side of the Church. In this case, the chatter only heightened from February 14 onward. In the aftermath of Francis's death, the initial days of mourning, the papal funeral, the *novendiales* (nine official days of mourning after the funeral), and the start of the daily meetings of the cardinals in the Vatican in the form of General Congregations, were all attended by speculation. Media attention focused on candidates who might be rising or falling as their fellow cardinals had a chance to assess them and get to know them better.

The General Congregations were especially important in the lead up to the conclave because many of the members of the College did not know each other. Pope Francis had brought the whole body of cardinals to Rome only infrequently. In 2015, he summoned the cardinals to discuss the reform of the Curia—that is, the Vatican bureaucracy—but the discussions soon became complicated over concerns surrounding the recent Synod on the Family and proposals regarding the possibility of admitting to Communion those Catholics who were divorced and remarried without receiving an annulment.

Francis did not bring them to Rome again until 2022, and that was a strictly controlled affair. The cardinals mainly received lectures on the reform of the Roman Curia and were given little opportunity to spend time together. In the meantime, Francis had been adding members to the

College in every year of his papacy save one—2021, due to COVID—and many of those new cardinals were from far-flung parts of the world.

This prompted some cardinals to call for a delay to the start of the conclave for the maximum amount of time allowed by the rules governing the interregnum. These are stated in the apostolic constitution *Universi dominici gregis*, promulgated by Pope St. John Paul II in 1996, and left essentially intact by his two immediate successors. Others, favoring a faster entry into the conclave, wanted to start as early as possible. In the end, the cardinals chose as a body to begin on the second day allowed by law.

Rising to the Top

Once underway, the General Congregations for the conclave were a forum for listening and speaking plainly on two broad questions: the immense challenges facing the Church and the profile of the person best suited to confront them as head of the Church. By the last General Congregation, the twelfth held on May 6—the day before the start of the conclave itself—the cardinals had spoken on a wide number of issues, with briefings and official statements from the Holy See Press Office highlighting some of the issues and priorities that emerged. As Vatican reporter Marco Mancini reported in ACI Stampa, they included:

1. Importance of Canon Law
2. Ethnic Diversity in the Church
3. Synodality and the Ecclesiology of Communion

4. A Pastoral Pontiff, Open to Dialogue with the World; the Missionary Nature of the Church; the Role of the Poor

5. Greater Focus on the Role of the Roman Curia

6. The Pursuit of Peace

7. Hermeneutics of Continuity Across the Last Three Pontificates[45]

Looking at the categories, cardinals were able to give sober commentary on the last twelve years of the pontificate of Pope Francis. Among them was a critique of Francis's decision to sever the link between power of governance in the Church and Holy Orders. As reported by the Jesuit publication *America*, Cardinal Beniamino Stella, age eighty-three and not an elector, spoke on April 30 at the seventh General Congregation and lamented that Pope Francis had "imposed his own ideas" on governance, especially in naming men and women not in Holy Orders to positions of authority in the Roman Curia. While creating a brief firestorm in the media, with some accusing Cardinal Stella of betraying Francis, who had named him a cardinal, the subsequent discussion challenged the assumption that the cardinals were looking for a carbon copy of the late pontiff.

To be sure, Francis had chosen 108 of the 133 cardinal electors who entered the Sistine Chapel, but the body was far more diverse, less ideological, and much more difficult to predict than expected by many experts. The voting cardinals came from seventy-one countries, and more than twenty were from countries being represented for the first time. Their interests did not easily map onto the categories used by Western media.

As with any conclave, names circulated in the media, and a short list of favorites and dark horses soon emerged. The list included: the Italians, Cardinal Pietro Parolin, the Secretary of State, and Cardinal Matteo Zuppi, the Archbishop of Bologna; the Filipino Cardinal Luis Tagle, Pro-Prefect of the Dicastery for Evangelization; the Spanish Cardinal Cristóbal López Romero, S.D.B., Archbishop of Rabat, Morocco; the Italian-born Cardinal Pierbattista Pizzaballa, Latin Patriarch of Jerusalem; the French Cardinal Jean-Marc Aveline, Archbishop of Marseille; and the Hungarian Cardinal Péter Erdő, Archbishop of Esztergom-Budapest, the major favorite among so-called conservative electors.

Soon after the start of the General Congregations, a few other names emerged as possible dark horse candidates, but one proved more enduring in the media and—it is now known—among the Cardinals themselves: Cardinal Robert Francis Prevost.

Prevost's elevation was not a media creation. In fact, he was openly mentioned as a would-be *papabile*—but he was easy to ignore because of the traditionally insurmountable problem that he was an American. Surely, it was said, the cardinals would not vote for a cardinal born in the United States, a citizen of the world's greatest superpower.

And yet, his name continued to circulate.

By the start of the conclave on May 7, a body of cardinal electors had coalesced around Prevost as their candidate. While the exact sequence of events that unfolded in the Sistine Chapel over the course of the four votes is not known (and will likely never be known) with certainty, Prevost arrived with votes and rapidly gained more votes until securing the required two-thirds majority on the fourth ballot, the first of the afternoon on May 8.

Once Cardinal Prevost surpassed the required vote of 89 cardinals, it is believed he kept going, to more than 100 of the 133 votes. He was then asked by Cardinal Pietro Parolin, the senior cardinal in the conclave, *Acceptasne electionem de te canonice factam in Summum Pontificem?* "Do you accept your canonical election as Supreme Pontiff?" He replied, *Accepto*. "I accept." He was then asked, *Quo nomine vis vocari?* "By what name do you wish to be called?" He replied, to the surprise of many of the cardinals, *Leone decimo quarto*: Leo XIV.

From Robert to Leo

How did the American Augustinian missionary win over the conclave? We can find some hint in a commentary written for the *New York Post* after the conclave by Cardinal Timothy Dolan of New York, who wrote:

> It had been a little more than two weeks since we had lost Pope Francis, and we still mourned his passing. But during the past 17 days, my brother cardinals and I had been meeting daily, discussing the strengths of the Church as we saw it from our perspective, the challenges we continue to face, and what kind of person we needed to lead us.
>
> During those many hours of meetings, at coffee breaks, or over lunch or dinner, I was often asked

by other cardinals, "Tell me about Cardinal Prevost. What kind of man is he?"

I had to reply that, in all honesty, I did not know him. I knew of him, of course, and what I had heard had impressed me greatly. A somewhat shy individual; a good listener; someone who spoke several languages; a priest with broad experience in Latin America; a former leader of his religious order; and, finally, someone who had spent the last few years in Rome, familiar with the workings of the bureaucracy that is the Roman Curia.

"He runs a good meeting," one cardinal said. Not a bad compliment, as most of us do not!

Another added, "he hears everyone out, but is able to make a decision when one is needed."

Still another, "he has a deep love for the poor."[46]

Dolan added that after spending a little time with Cardinal Prevost, he came away impressed. And he was not the only one.

In assessing how the cardinals might vote, two criteria established themselves in discussions during the General Congregations. The first hinged on how a prospective new pope might fall on the major issues facing the Church. Would a candidate be able to respond in a compelling way to the issues and concerns that had emerged from the General Congregations?

The second, related to the first but also crucial in its own right, was the question of whether the new pope would be able to bridge the divisions that were apparent in the Church—and manifest among the cardinals themselves—both during and in the aftermath of the pontificate of Pope Francis. This was tied to the issue of continuity, and whether the next pope would push aggressively for a continuation of the program of Francis in such key areas as "synodality," or steer a path sharply away from Francis, or find a middle course, guiding the Church ahead in light of not only Francis's pontificate but all of the pontificates in the modern era, especially after the Second Vatican Council (1962–1965).

Looking at the issues discussed by the cardinals in the General Congregations, Cardinal Prevost's experience and character responded to nearly every topic on the table. He was a canon lawyer who could help to clarify many of the points of confusion or uncertainty created by the tidal wave of new laws and changes to canon law made by the late pontiff. He understood authentic diversity in the Church through his years in service, especially in Latin America and as head of the Augustinians, while also being absolutely committed — per his episcopal motto — to unity in Christ.

He supported synodality but in a measured way. He understood intensely the missionary nature of the Church. He had a firm understanding of the Roman Curia and the need for good governance. He had a reputation for listening and finding consensus as a path to authentic peace. And he grasped the importance of continuity, having served under multiple pontificates.

There remained the question of his American heritage. Robert Prevost was born in the United States, but the Cardinals realized that he had not only been away from his native country for decades, but possessed dual citizenship in the United States and Peru. Aside from being a natural-born American citizen, Leo is a naturalized citizen of Peru, an honor accorded to all Catholic bishops by virtue of a concordat with the Holy See. In addition, as a cardinal serving in Rome, he also held a Vatican passport, granting him what is traditionally called "functional citizenship" in the Holy See.

He loved Peru and stood as a builder of bridges—between North and South America and potentially between the United States and Rome. He also built bridges from among cardinals across the ideological spectrum by his reputation for taking a measured and careful approach to the most vexing internal issues facing the Church.

In the end, the fact that Cardinal Robert Prevost was from the United States had little impact on the decisions of the cardinal electors. In their press conference at the North American College in Rome after the conclave, the American cardinals were asked about the impact of Pope Leo's birthplace. Cardinal Robert McElroy, Archbishop of Washington, expressed surprise that it was not a key question. "I think," he said, "the impact of him being an American was almost negligible in the deliberations of the conclave, and surprisingly so." Cardinal Daniel DiNardo, Archbishop Emeritus of Galveston-Houston, added, "he's really a citizen of the entire world since he has spent so much of his life, ministry, missionary work and zeal for Christ in South America."[47]

Cardinal Prevost was elected to the papacy by most of the cardinal electors who saw in him the man most worthy to become the 266th successor of St. Peter. He was not a compromise candidate. He was a consensus of who the Church needs at this moment. His gratitude to the cardinals was readily acknowledged by the newly elected Leo XIV the day after his election:

> You, dear Cardinals, are the closest collaborators of the Pope. This has proved a great comfort to me in accepting a yoke clearly far beyond my own limited powers, as it would be for any of us. Your presence reminds me that the Lord, who has entrusted me with this mission, will not leave me alone in bearing its responsibility.[48]

In a particular way, Leo will rely on St. Augustine, and the Augustinian spirituality that has sustained him throughout his life and ministry. This can be seen in one particular quotation, which Leo has repeated, from his great forebear. Here, Augustine acknowledges his fear and weakness as a spiritual leader — but places his trust in his shared identity with his flock in the Divine Person of Jesus Christ. This is the model Pope Leo XIV is taking for his own spiritual leadership:

> What I am *for* you terrified me; what I am *with* you consoles me. *For* you I am a bishop; but *with* you I am a Christian. The former is a duty; the latter a grace. The former is a danger; the latter, salvation. (St. Augustine, Sermon 340)

Conclusion: A New Leonine Age

WHAT'S IN A NAME? In Genesis, the power to name the animals, given to Adam and Eve, signified their dominion over God's lesser creatures. When parents name their children, they're giving them their first identity, and in the case of some names, like saints' names, expressing their hopes for their future.

A pope chooses his own name — but not by himself. Just as the cardinals in the conclave respond to the Holy Spirit, even if they don't fully realize how they're doing so, the new Holy Father also interacts with the Spirit. It may not be that the Holy Spirit directly moved Cardinal Robert Francis Prevost to select Leo; it may be that the Spirit delivered to the Church just the right man who would choose Leo, regardless.

In any event, the Lord, the Church, and the Vicar of Christ are telling us something important about our age by inaugurating a new Leonine era.

A Tradition of Greatness

While much commentary (including in this book) has been dedicated to Leo XIV's immediate Leonine predecessor, Leo XIII, and the new Leo has appealed to Leo XIII directly on multiple occasions, it would be a mistake to ignore the very first Leo, in whose tradition every future one has followed.

Pope St. Leo I, also known as Leo the Great, was one of the most important pontiffs in Church history — a sentiment expressed by Pope Benedict XVI himself. He is most famous today for leaving Rome in 452 to appeal to Attila the Hun, who had invaded Italy and was marching toward the Eternal City. While we don't know what was said between Leo and Attila, we do know what happened: the conqueror packed up and left the Italian peninsula. The dreaded ruler of the Huns, called the Scourge of God, died soon after.

But Leo's greatest achievements were theological. He was instrumental in defining Christ's fully human and fully divine natures as a "hypostatic union" in a single person — a complicated concept for another time. It can be hard to place ourselves in the mindset of the fifth century, but at that time debates about Christ's nature roiled the nascent Christian world, and it was unclear which understanding would win out.

Leo's submission to the Council of Chalcedon in 451 was brilliant and, best of all, true, and it defines the Church's Christological doctrine to this day. For this, Leo was proclaimed a Doctor of the Church, and one of only two popes, with St. Gregory the Great, to be accorded that honor. It was also under Leo the Great that the idea of the preeminence of the bishop of Rome — that is, as the pope — was crystallized, and then settled to this day and beyond.

It was in this great tradition that Cardinal Gioacchino Pecci took Leo XIII as his papal name in February 1878. Leo XIV is intentionally echoing Leo XIII in applying the Church's social teachings to a contemporary technological, economic, and social revolution: then, the industrial age; now, the digital age.

In a speech to the members of the Centesimus Annus Pro Pontifice Foundation in the Vatican on May 17, 2025, Pope Leo spoke of the central role of Catholic social teaching in confronting the needs of today—faithful to Leo XIII and *Rerum novarum* as well as the Second Vatican Council. "I invite you," he said to the group but, with a voice speaking to the entire Church,

> to participate actively and creatively in this discernment process, and thus contribute, with all of God's people, to the development of the Church's social doctrine in this age of significant social changes, listening to everyone and engaging in dialogue with all. In our day, there is a widespread thirst for justice, a desire for authentic fatherhood and motherhood, a profound longing for spirituality, especially among young people and the marginalized, who do not always find effective means of making their needs known. There is a growing demand for the Church's social doctrine, to which we need to respond.[49]

The new Leo is likely to upset nearly every political and ideological faction at one time or another, just as Leo XIII did, by asserting the timeless nature of Christian thought, which transcends all our contemporary categories. But there are other resonances between these two men—other areas where the new Leo seems poised to continue his predecessor's legacy.

For instance, Leo XIII famously encouraged a revival of reading and celebrating the theology of St. Thomas Aquinas. The legacy of this Thomistic renaissance continues to this day, with Aquinas enshrined in a preeminent role among theologians across Church history. Leo XIII founded the Pontifical Academy of St. Thomas Aquinas, as well as the faculties of philosophy and canon law at the Pontifical University of St. Thomas Aquinas. Nearly a century later, of course, Leo XIV would receive his doctorate in canon law from the latter institution.

It seems possible, if not likely, that Leo XIV will aim to do for St. Augustine—known as the Doctor of Grace—what Leo XIII did for St. Thomas, as the theologian James K. A. Smith put it for *America*. Already, the new Leo has appealed to the great Augustine on several occasions, and he has visited with his confreres at the Augustinianum. It may be, in fact, that just as the world needed the precision and breadth of St. Thomas in the days of Leo XIII, the world needs the humaneness and depth of St. Augustine, especially in his theology of communion, in the days of Leo XIV. Or, as Dr. Smith put it: "I'm not sure our world needs us to parse arcane metaphysics at this moment. I think the world needs to hear that God is near to the broken-hearted and offers his own body to satisfy our longings."[50]

One more thing about Pope Leo XIII, which may prove important to Pope Leo XIV in a world, especially in the West, where superstition and the occult are making a comeback: he composed the beautiful and strong Prayer to St. Michael the Archangel, which is being heard more and more in churches today.

Bringing Together

The pontificate of Pope Leo XIV is still only days old. And yet, there is a sense of clarity and mission about it that began from his walk onto the world stage on May 8. Among the reasons for the sense of certainty and immediate stability is the deliberate decision he made to dress in the traditional vesture of the popes, adding to the papal white cassock and pellegrina the red mozzetta and stole. This was not a rejection of the deliberate simplicity of Pope Francis but a conscious effort to connect himself—and with it his pontificate—to his predecessors and the long customs and symbols of the papacy and the Church.

This drawing of a line of continuity and integration goes far beyond the merely symbolic or sartorial. There is a manifest desire to achieve the integration of recent pontificates, the Second Vatican Council, and the Fathers of the Church. This is not some effort to placate perceived factions or camps in some ecclesiastical power struggle. Rather, it is mining the rich treasures of teaching that characterized the great Fathers, the Council, and the modern popes to build unity in the Church in a fractured era. Pope Leo XIV believes that these teachings can impel the Church toward unity rooted in Christ and prepare all of us for the immense task of evangelization to which we are all called.

This integration has been on display since the first *Urbi et Orbi* blessing on May 8 and has continued virtually every day since. It is obvious in the use of references in his public speaking and preaching to the Second Vatican Council (especially the seminal documents *Lumen gentium* and *Gaudium et spes*);

to Church Fathers, including Augustine, Pope St. Gregory the Great, Ephrem the Syrian, and Ignatius of Antioch; and to all his recent predecessors.

Fr. Thomas Joseph White, O.P., the rector magnificus of the Pontifical University of St. Thomas Aquinas in Rome, wrote in his commentary for *First Things*, "A Leonine Revival," on the particular use of the modern popes:

> Perhaps there is something to learn, then, from each of the pontificates, in search of a more comprehensive unity: from St. John Paul II, his evangelical witness to the teaching and practice of the Catholic faith, in ways that were radical and sometimes counter-cultural in the face of a secularized world; from Benedict, the search for a deeper liturgical life in the Church and his commitment to scholarship and theological reflection; from Francis, his message of universal mercy, his concrete and policy-oriented solidarity with the poor, his consultation of the faithful, and his outreach to those previously alienated from the Church's hierarchy.[51]

Like these and many other predecessors in their times, Pope Leo XIV faces a host of challenges at the start of his pontificate. Today, they include war in Ukraine and Gaza and elsewhere; the technological revolutions and the threat to the human person; growing secularism and atheism and the hatred of religious belief; mass migration and the quest for work and dignity; social and cultural fragmentation; threats to the family and human life from gender ideology, abortion, euthanasia, and surrogacy; and divisions within the Church, most conspicuously the German Synodal Way and its heterodox enterprise for the Church in Germany.

Our new Holy Father seems convinced that the road ahead for the Church and the world will be paved by hearing and applying the timeless teachings of the Church in new situations and circumstances. This is why he is so consciously integrating Augustinian and Leonine thought in a deeply Christocentric way.

Through Him, with Him, in Him

> We traverse in spirit and thought the wide expanse of ocean; and although We have at other times addressed you in writing... yet have We now resolved to speak to you separately, trusting that We shall be, God willing, of some assistance to the Catholic cause amongst you. To this We apply Ourselves with the utmost zeal and care; because We highly esteem and love exceedingly the young and vigorous American nation, in which We plainly discern latent forces for the advancement alike of civilization and of Christianity.

This is how Pope Leo XIII began his encyclical *Longinqua*, "On Catholicism in the United States," the document with which this book began. How beautiful it is that the love he expressed for America might be returned in the person of Pope Leo XIV.

And yet the America the former Leo addressed was very different from the one in which the new Leo grew up. While the United States is still, in world-historical terms, a young nation, it has matured significantly in the 130 years since the encyclical.

In 1895, Leo XIII could describe the "latent forces" that could nurture the Church in America. By the time Robert Prevost was born in Chicago in 1955, those forces had done their work, and the Church was in full bloom. Places like Dolton and Riverdale were defined by their parishes, which were the center not just of spiritual life but of social and even political life. Catholic culture permeated the *saeculum*, meaning there was no real secular sphere, at least in the sense we understand it today.

During Leo XIV's lifetime, that all went away. His parish and schools folded and were abandoned. Dolton and Riverdale and much of the rest of the South Side fell into decline. Catholic culture became cultural Catholicism, with the identity maintained and its source — Christ and His Church — often left behind. In their place have rushed materialism and consumerism and utilitarianism, which have promised to not only replace but improve upon the truth and peace of Christ.

And, of course, they have failed. People are anxious and miserable, their hearts more restless than ever. Leo, the first American pope, has witnessed this process firsthand.

But this is not his only intimate experience of the Church and the People of God, and of what threatens them. If America has shown that the promises of modernity are empty, Peru showed that the path to a faithless modernity is not inevitable. There, Leo witnessed great material poverty — which he worked to alleviate — married to great spiritual richness. And so he would have seen and learned that attempts to compromise with secular modernity would offer nothing but despair to the people he served.

And to the extent the values of the modern secular West seeped into his communities in Peru, especially through the mass media, he would have seen the same process beginning there that dissolved the institutions of the Church in his hometown: the false promises of materialism and ideology. This process he would identify as a kind of new colonialism, trying to mold traditional cultures into modern secular ones not by the sword but by the smartphone.

Or, rather, he might say—and essentially did say in his 2012 intervention at the Synod on the New Evangelization—that the missionary Church must combat the secular missionary messaging of the mass media.

Chicago. Peru. Rome. Pastor. Teacher. Missionary. Prior general. Bishop. Cardinal. Pope Leo XIV has seen and experienced the Church in more contexts than perhaps any other person currently living. He understands that the needs of the People of God are, in many respects, quite different in each of those contexts. He knows that the Church must be responsive to those needs in a nimble and humble way.

But, most of all, to repeat some of Leo's most important words from earlier in this book, "the underlying challenge that Christ left to us to preach the Gospel and that *this is the same everywhere*" [emphasis added].

What Pope Leo XIV, following the great St. Augustine himself, will bring to the papacy is an uncompromising emphasis on the Divine Person of Jesus Christ. This is the same everywhere, because He is the same everywhere. He is the One whom everybody needs, whether they are materially poor or spiritually parched. He is the only principle of unity that can unite Chicago and Peru and Rome and every place and every person in between.

In illo Uno unum. In the One, we are one. That, more than anything else, is what Pope Leo XIV believes the world needs to know today.

Afterword

Homily from the Mass of the Beginning of the Petrine Ministry of Pope Leo XIV

Sunday, May 18, 2025.

I GREET ALL OF you with a heart full of gratitude at the beginning of the ministry that has been entrusted to me. Saint Augustine wrote: "Lord, you have made us for yourself, and our heart is restless until it rests in you" (*Confessions*, I:1,1).

In these days, we have experienced intense emotions. The death of Pope Francis filled our hearts with sadness. In those difficult hours, we felt like the crowds that the Gospel says were "like sheep without a shepherd" (*Mt* 9:36). Yet on Easter Sunday, we received his final blessing and, in the light of the resurrection, we experienced the days that followed in the certainty that the Lord never abandons his people, but gathers them when they are scattered and guards them "as a shepherd guards his flock" (*Jer* 31:10).

In this spirit of faith, the College of Cardinals met for the conclave. Coming from different backgrounds and experiences, we placed in God's hands our desire to elect the new Successor of Peter, the Bishop of Rome, a shepherd capable of preserving the rich heritage of the Christian faith and, at the same time, looking to the future, in order to confront the questions, concerns, and challenges of today's world. Accompanied by your prayers, we could feel the working of the Holy Spirit, who was able to bring us into harmony, like musical instruments, so that our heartstrings could vibrate in a single melody.

I was chosen, without any merit of my own, and now, with fear and trembling, *I come to you as a brother*, who desires to be the servant of your faith and your joy, walking with you on the path of God's love, for he wants us all to be united in one family. *Love and unity*: these are the two dimensions of the mission entrusted to Peter by Jesus.

We see this in today's Gospel, which takes us to the Sea of Galilee, where Jesus began the mission he received from the Father: to be a "fisher" of humanity in order to draw it up from the waters of evil and death. Walking along the shore, he had called Peter and the other first disciples to be, like him, "fishers of men." Now, after the resurrection, it is up to them to carry on this mission, to cast their nets again and again, to bring the hope of the Gospel into the "waters" of the world, to sail the seas of life so that all may experience God's embrace.

How can Peter carry out this task? The Gospel tells us that it is possible only because his own life was touched by the infinite and unconditional love of God, even in the hour of his failure and denial. For this reason, when Jesus addresses Peter, the Gospel uses the Greek verb *agapáo*, which refers to the love that God has for us, to the offering of himself without reserve and without calculation. Whereas the verb used in Peter's response describes the love of friendship that we have for one another.

Consequently, when Jesus asks Peter, "Simon, son of John, do you love me more than these?" (*Jn* 21:16), he is referring to the love of the Father. It is as if Jesus said to him, "Only if you have known and experienced this love of God, which never fails, will you be able to feed my lambs. Only in the love of God the Father will you be able to love your brothers and sisters with that same 'more,' that is, by offering your life for your brothers and sisters."

Peter is thus entrusted with the task of "loving more" and giving his life for the flock. The ministry of Peter is distinguished precisely by this self-sacrificing love, because the Church of Rome presides in charity and its true authority is the charity of Christ. It is never a question of capturing others by force, by religious propaganda or by means of power. Instead, it is always and only a question of loving as Jesus did.

The Apostle Peter himself tells us that Jesus "is the stone that was rejected by you, the builders, and has become the cornerstone" (*Acts* 4:11). Moreover, if the rock is Christ, Peter must shepherd the flock without ever yielding to the temptation to be an autocrat, lording it over those entrusted to him (cf. *1 Pet* 5:3). On the contrary, he is called to serve the faith of his brothers and sisters, and to walk alongside them, for all of us are "living stones" (*1 Pet* 2:5), called through our baptism to build God's house in fraternal communion, in the harmony of the Spirit, in the coexistence of diversity. In the words of Saint Augustine: "The Church consists of all those who are in harmony with their brothers and sisters and who love their neighbor" (Serm. 359, 9).

Brothers and sisters, I would like that our first great desire be for *a united Church, a sign of unity and communion, which becomes a leaven for a reconciled world.* In this our time, we still see too much discord, too many wounds caused by hatred, violence, prejudice, the fear of difference, and an economic paradigm that exploits the Earth's resources and marginalizes the poorest. For our part, we want to be a small leaven of unity, communion and fraternity within the world. We want to say to the world, with humility and joy: Look to Christ! Come closer to him! Welcome his word that enlightens and consoles! Listen to his offer of love and become his one family: *in the one Christ, we are one.* This is the path to follow together, among ourselves but also with our sister Christian churches, with those who follow other religious paths, with those who are searching for God, with all women and men of good will, in order to build a new world where peace reigns!

This is the missionary spirit that must animate us; not closing ourselves off in our small groups, nor feeling superior to the world. We are called to offer God's love to everyone, in order to achieve that unity which does not cancel out differences but values the personal history of each person and the social and religious culture of every people.

Brothers and sisters, this is the hour for love! The heart of the Gospel is the love of God that makes us brothers and sisters. With my predecessor Leo XIII, we can ask ourselves today: If this criterion "were to prevail in the world, would not every conflict cease and peace return?" (*Rerum Novarum*, 21).

With the light and the strength of the Holy Spirit, let us build a Church founded on God's love, a sign of unity, a missionary Church that opens its arms to the world, proclaims the word, allows itself to be made "restless" by history, and becomes a leaven of harmony for humanity.

Together, as one people, as brothers and sisters, let us walk towards God and love one another.

Endnotes

1. Leo XIV, Apostolic Blessing *Urbi et Orbi* (May 8, 2025).
2. Leo XIII, encyclical letter *Longinqua* (On Catholicism in the United States) (January 6, 1895), no. 13.
3. Leo XIII, *Longinqua*, no. 5.
4. Leo XIII, *Longinqua*, no. 4.
5. Leo XIV, Address to the College of Cardinals (May 10, 2025).
6. Vatican Council II, Pastoral Consistution on the Church in the Modern World *Gaudium et spes* (December 7, 1965), no. 26.
7. Leo XIV, Homily (May 9, 2025).
8. David Vergun, "Pope Leo XIV's Father Served in the Navy during World War II," U.S. Department of Defense, May 9, 2025, accessed May 19, 2025, https://www.defense.gov/News/News-Stories/Article/Article/4180629/pope-leo-xivs-father-served-in-the-navy-during-world-war-ii/.
9. Richard Fausset and Robert Chiarito, "New Pope Has Creole Roots in New Orleans," *New York Times*, May

10, 2025, accessed May 19, 2025, https://www.nytimes.com/2025/05/08/us/pope-leo-creole-new-orleans.html.

10 Julie Bosman, "The Mother Whose Catholic Faith Inspired the Future Pope," *New York Times*, May 11, 2025, accessed May 19, 2025, https://www.nytimes.com/2025/05/11/us/mildred-prevost-robert-pope-leo-xiv-mother.html.

11 Max Marin et al., "Inside Villanova in the 1970s, When the Future Peope Leo XIV Arrived on Campus," *Philadelphia Inquirer*, May 10, 2025, accessed May 19, 2025, https://www.union-bulletin.com/news/national/inside-villanova-in-the-1970s-when-the-future-pope-leo-xiv-arrived-on-campus/article_9fc6b56a-70f0-5830-90cb-c47da8e4b74a.html.

12 Jonathan Liedl, "Visiting Pope Leo XIV's Chicago: How the South Side Shaped America's First Pontiff," *National Catholic Register*, May 12, 2025, accessed May 19, 2025, https://www.ncregister.com/news/visiting-pope-leo-xiv-s-chicago-neighborhood.

13 Pope Leo XIV, Address to the College of Cardinals (May 10, 2025).

14 Quoted in Ricardo Morales Jiménez, "Cardinal Prevost's Warning in the Face of Polarization," *LaCroix*, May 10, 2025, accessed May 19, 2025, https://international.la-croix.com/opinions/cardinal-prevosts-warning-in-the-face-of-polarization.

15 Matthew Becklo, "Pope Leo XIV: 'A Son of St. Augustine,'" *National Catholic Register*, May 12, 2025, accessed May

19, 2025, https://www.ncregister.com/commentaries/pope-leo-xiv-a-son-of-st-augustine.

16 "Pope Leo XIV Started His Papal Journey in St. Louis," *St. Louis Post-Dispatch*, May 8, 2025, accessed May 19, 2025, https://www.stltoday.com/news/local/metro/article_89d4062b-75e0-495e-8b30-a91e8a0ac920.html.

17 "Venerable Joseph Batholomew Menochio: Augustinian Sevant of God," Midwest Augustinians, accessed May 19, 2025, https://www.midwestaugustinians.org/joseph-menochio.

18 Mike Aquilina, "Pope Leo XIV's Motto, Drawn from St. Augustine, Speaks Volumes to This Moment," *National Catholic Register*, May 12, 2025, accessed May 19, 2025, https://www.ncregister.com/commentaries/aquilina-pope-leo-xiv-motto.

19 Ricardo Morales Jiménez, "Interview with Cardinal Robert Prevost OSA: 'Above All, a Bishop Must Proclaim Jesus Christ,'" Order of Saint Augustine, updated May 8, 2025, accessed May 19, 2025, https://www.augustinianorder.org/post/interview-with-cardinal-robert-prevost-osa-above-all-a-bishop-must-proclaim-jesus-christ.

20 Aquilina, "Pope Leo XIV's Motto."

21 Jiménez, "Interview with Cardinal Robert Prevost."

22 Leo XIV, Apostolic Blessing *Urbi et Orbi*.

23 Kevin Clarke, "A Missionary Pope: What Pope Leo XIV's Years in Peru Tell Us about How He'll Lead the Church," *America*, May 13, 2025, accessed May 19, 2025, https://

www.americamagazine.org/faith/2025/05/13/pope-let-xiv-peru-chiclayo-trujillo-chulucanas-turley-flaherty-augustinian-250678.

24 Ibid.

25 Motoko Rich, "There's Never Been a Pope From the U.S. Could This Cardinal Change That?" *New York Times*, updated May 8, 2025, accessed May 19, 2025, https://www.nytimes.com/2025/05/02/world/americas/pope-candidate-cardinal-robert-francis-prevost.html.

26 Franklin Briceño and Nicole Winfield, "Prevost, Now Pope Leo XIV, Known as the 'Saint of the North' in Peru for His Closeness to Poor," Associated Press, May 8, 2025, accessed May 19, 2025, https://apnews.com/article/prevost-american-pope-profile-leo-xiv-f9d14d75ae3b-be50bda121f27ee0e42b.

27 Ines San Martin, "In Boots during Floods, in Vestments at Mass: Peruvians Claim Leo XIV as a Local," OSV News, May 14, 2025, accessed May 19, 2025, https://www.osvnews.com/in-boots-during-floods-in-vestments-at-mass-peruvians-claim-leo-xiv-as-a-local.

28 Ibid.

29 Walter Sánchez Silva, "Peruvian Bishop Defends Pope Leo XIV against Accusation of Cover-Up," Catholic News Agency, May 13, 2025, accessed May 19, 2025, https://www.catholicnewsagency.com/news/264073/peruvian-bishop-defends-pope-leo-xiv-against-accusations-of-cover-up.

30 Ibid.

31 Andrea Tornielli, "Archbishop Prevost: 'The Bishop Is a Pastor, Not a Manager,' " Vatican News, May 4, 2023, accessed May 19, 2025, https://www.vaticannews.va/en/vatican-city/news/2023-05/archbishop-prevost-the-bishop-is-a-pastor-not-a-manager.html.

32 *Eucharistic Miracle of Eten: Peru, 1649*, accessed May 19, 2025, http://www.therealpresence.org/eucharst/mir/english_pdf/Eten.pdf.

33 Ibid.

34 Mitra Taj, Julie Turkewitz, and Genevieve Glatsky, "In Chiclayo, Peru, Locals Cheer the 'Peruvian Pope'," *New York Times*, May 9, 2025, accessed May 19, 2025, https://www.nytimes.com/2025/05/09/world/europe/pope-peru-reaction.html.

35 Rhina Guidos, "Few Know Pope Leo XIV like These Augustinian Sisters from Peru's Catholic Community," Global Sisters Report, May 9, 2025, accessed May 19, 2025, https://www.globalsistersreport.org/religious-life/few-know-pope-leo-xiv-these-augustinian-sisters-perus-catholic-community.

36 Jiménez, "Interview with Cardinal Robert Prevost."

37 Matthew McDonald, "Pope Leo XIV Is First Missionary to Become Pope in a Long, Long Time," *National Catholic Register*, May 14, 2025, accessed May 19, 2025, https://www.ewtnvatican.com/articles/pope-leo-xvi-is-first-missionary-to-become-pope-in-a-long-long-time-5395.

38 Clarke, "A Missionary Pope."
39 Jiménez, "Interview with Cardinal Robert Prevost."
40 Leo XIV, Address to Participants in the Jubilee of Oriental Churches (May 14, 2025).
41 McDonald, "Pope Leo XIV Is First Missionary."
42 Guidos, "Few Know Pope Leo XIV like These Augustinian Sisters."
43 Cindy Wooden, "Unity, Not Nationality Led to Pope Leo's Election, U.S. Cardinals Say," USCCB, May 9, 2025, accessed May 19, 2025, https://www.usccb.org/news/2025/unity-not-nationality-led-pope-leos-election-us-cardinals-say.
44 Leo XIV, Address to the Representatives of the Media (May 12, 2025).
45 Marco Mancini, "7 Priorities for the Next Pope, According to the Cardinals" National Catholic Register, May 7, 2025, accessed May 19, 2025, https://www.ncregister.com/blog/seven-themes-twelve-congregations.
46 Timothy Cardinal Dolan, "Cardinal Dolan Reveals How Pope Leo XIV 'Impressed' Him at the Conclave—and Predicts What Kind of Pontiff He Will Be," New York Post, May 10, 2025, accessed May 19, 2025, https://nypost.com/2025/05/10/world-news/cardinal-dolan-reveals-how-future-pope-leo-xiv-impressed-him-at-the-conclave-and-predicts-what-kind-of-pontiff-he-will-be/?utm_campaign=nypost&utm_medium=referral.
47 Wooden, "Unity, Not Nationality"

48 Leo XIV, Address of His Holiness Pope Leo XIV to the College of Cardinals (May, 10, 2025).

49 Leo XIV, "Address of His Holiness Pope Leo XIV to Members of the 'Centesimus Annus Pro Pontifice' Foundation" (May 17, 2025).

50 James K. A. Smith, "What to Expect from an Augustinian Pope," *America*, May 12, 2025, accessed May 19, 2025, https://www.americamagazine.org/faith/2025/05/12/smith-augustinian-pope-leo-250662.

51 Thomas Joseph White, "A Leonine Revival," *First Things*, May 13, 2025, accessed May 19, 2025, https://firstthings.com/a-leonine-revival/

About the Author

MATTHEW BUNSON IS VICE President and Editorial Director of EWTN News and an award-winning Catholic journalist and writer. A veteran of Catholic media for more than thirty years, he is the author or co-author of fifty-six books including *The Encyclopedia of Catholic History*, *The Encyclopedia of Saints*, and the first biography of Pope Francis in the English language in 2013.